HBase Essentials

A practical guide to realizing the seamless potential
of storing and managing high-volume, high-velocity
data quickly and painlessly with HBase

Nishant Garg

BIRMINGHAM - MUMBAI

HBase Essentials

First published: November 2014

Production reference: 1071114

Published by Packt Publishing Ltd.
Livery Place
35 Livery Street
Birmingham B3 2PB, UK.

ISBN 978-1-78398-724-5

www.packtpub.com

Cover image by Gerard Eykhoff (gerard@eykhoff.nl)

Credits

Author
Nishant Garg

Reviewers
Kiran Gangadharan
Andrea Mostosi
Eric K. Wong

Commissioning Editor
Akram Hussain

Acquisition Editor
Vinay Argekar

Content Development Editors
Shaon Basu
Rahul Nair

Technical Editor
Anand Singh

Copy Editors
Dipti Kapadia
Deepa Nambiar

Project Coordinator
Aboli Ambardekar

Proofreaders
Paul Hindle
Linda Morris

Indexer
Rekha Nair

Graphics
Ronak Dhruv
Abhinash Sahu

Production Coordinator
Conidon Miranda

Cover Work
Conidon Miranda

About the Author

Nishant Garg has over 14 years of experience in software architecture and development in various technologies such as Java, Java Enterprise Edition, SOA, Spring, Hibernate, Hadoop, Hive, Flume, Sqoop, Oozie, Spark, Shark, YARN, Impala, Kafka, Storm, Solr/Lucene, and NoSQL databases including HBase, Cassandra, MongoDB, and MPP Databases such as GreenPlum.

He received his MS degree in Software Systems from Birla Institute of Technology and Science, Pilani, India, and is currently working as a technical architect in Big Data R&D Group in Impetus Infotech Pvt. Ltd.

Nishant, in his previous experience, has enjoyed working with the most recognizable names in IT services and financial industries, employing full software life cycle methodologies such as Agile and Scrum. He has also undertaken many speaking engagements on Big Data Technologies and is also the author of *Apache Kafka, Packt Publishing*.

I would like to thank my parents, Shri. Vishnu Murti Garg and Smt. Vimla Garg, for their continuous encouragement and motivation throughout my life. I would also like to say thanks to my wife, Himani, and my kids, Nitigya and Darsh, for their never-ending support, which keeps me going.

Finally, I would like to say thanks to Vineet Tyagi, head of Innovation Labs, Impetus Technologies, and Dr. Vijay, Director of Technology, Innovation Labs, Impetus Technologies, for having faith in me and giving me an opportunity to write.

About the Reviewers

Kiran Gangadharan works as a software writer at WalletKit, Inc. He has been passionate about computers since childhood and has 3 years of professional experience. He loves to work on open source projects and read about various technologies/architectures. Apart from programming, he enjoys the pleasure of a good cup of coffee and reading a thought-provoking book. He has also reviewed *Instant Node.js Starter*, *Pedro Teixeira*, *Packt Publishing*.

Andrea Mostosi is a technology enthusiast. He has been an innovation lover since childhood. He started working in 2003 and has worked on several projects, playing almost every role in the computer science environment. He is currently the CTO at The Fool, a company that tries to make sense of web and social data. During his free time, he likes traveling, running, cooking, biking, and coding.

> I would like to thank my geek friends: Simone M, Daniele V, Luca T, Luigi P, Michele N, Luca O, Luca B, Diego C, and Fabio B. They are the smartest people I know, and comparing myself with them has always pushed me to be better.

Eric K. Wong started with computing as a childhood hobby. He developed his own BBS on C64 in the early 80s and ported it to Linux in the early 90s. He started working in 1996 where he cut his teeth on SGI IRIX and HPC, which has shaped his focus on performance tuning and large clusters. In 1998, he started speaking, teaching, and consulting on behalf of a wide array of vendors. He remains an avid technology enthusiast and lives in Vancouver, Canada. He maintains a blog at `http://www.masterschema.com`.

www.PacktPub.com

Support files, eBooks, discount offers, and more

For support files and downloads related to your book, please visit www.PacktPub.com.

Did you know that Packt offers eBook versions of every book published, with PDF and ePub files available? You can upgrade to the eBook version at www.PacktPub.com and as a print book customer, you are entitled to a discount on the eBook copy. Get in touch with us at service@packtpub.com for more details.

At www.PacktPub.com, you can also read a collection of free technical articles, sign up for a range of free newsletters and receive exclusive discounts and offers on Packt books and eBooks.

http://PacktLib.PacktPub.com

Do you need instant solutions to your IT questions? PacktLib is Packt's online digital book library. Here, you can search, access, and read Packt's entire library of books.

Why subscribe?

- Fully searchable across every book published by Packt
- Copy and paste, print, and bookmark content
- On demand and accessible via a web browser

Free access for Packt account holders

If you have an account with Packt at www.PacktPub.com, you can use this to access PacktLib today and view 9 entirely free books. Simply use your login credentials for immediate access.

Table of Contents

Preface

Apache HBase is an open source distributed, Big Data store that scales to billions of rows and columns. HBase sits on top of clusters of commodity machines.

This book is here to help you get familiar with HBase and use it to solve your challenges related to storing a large amount of data. It is aimed at getting you started with programming with HBase so that you will have a solid foundation to build on about the different types of advanced features and usages.

What this book covers

Chapter 1, *Introducing HBase*, introduces HBase to the developers and provides the steps required to set up the HBase cluster in the local and pseudo-distributed modes. It also explains briefly the basic building blocks of the HBase cluster and the commands used to play with HBase.

Chapter 2, *Defining the Schema*, this answers some basic questions such as how data modeling is approached and how tables are designed in the first half of the chapter. The next half provides the examples of CRUD operations in HBase using the Java-based developers API provided by HBase.

Chapter 3, *Advanced Data Modeling*, takes the concepts discussed in the previous chapter into more depth. It explains the role of different keys in HBase and later picks up advanced features such as table scan and filters in detail.

Chapter 4, *The HBase Architecture*, provides an insight into the HBase architecture. It covers how data is stored and replicated internally in HBase. It also discusses how to secure HBase access and explains HBase and MapReduce over Hadoop integration in detail.

Chapter 5, *The HBase Advanced API*, shares the advanced features such as counters, coprocessors, and their usage using the HBase developers' API. It also discusses the API available for the HBase administration.

Chapter 6, *HBase Clients*, discusses in detail various clients that are available for HBase. The HBase client list includes HBase shell, Kundera, REST clients, Thrift client, and Hadoop ecosystem clients.

Chapter 7, *HBase Administration*, focuses on HBase administration. It provides details about the HBase cluster management, monitoring, and performance tuning. In the end, it talks about cluster troubleshooting.

What you need for this book

The basic list of software required for this book is as follows:

- CentOS 6.5 64 bit
- Oracle JDK SE 7 (Java Development Kit Standard Edition)
- HBase 0.96.2
- Hadoop 2.2.0
- ZooKeeper 3.4.5

Who this book is for

This book is for readers who want to know about Apache HBase at a hands-on level; the key audience is those with software development experience but no prior exposure to Apache HBase or similar technologies.

This book is also for enterprise application developers and Big Data enthusiasts who have worked with other NoSQL database systems and now want to explore Apache HBase as another futuristic scalable solution.

Conventions

In this book, you will find a number of styles of text that distinguish between different kinds of information. Here are some examples of these styles, and an explanation of their meaning.

Code words in text, database table names, folder names, filenames, file extensions, pathnames, dummy URLs, user input, and Twitter handles are shown as follows: "Data deletion in HBase can happen for a single row or in the form of a batch representing multiple rows using the following method of the HTable class."

A block of code is set as follows:

```
List<Delete> deletes = new ArrayList<Delete>();
Delete delete1 = new Delete(Bytes.toBytes("row-1"));
delete1.deleteColumn(Bytes.toBytes("cf1"), Bytes.toBytes("greet"));
deletes.add(delete1);
```

Any command-line input or output is written as follows:

```
[root@localhost hbase-0.98.7-hadoop2]# bin/hbase shell
hbase(main):001:0> help 'create'
```

New terms and **important words** are shown in bold. Words that you see on the screen, in menus or dialog boxes for example, appear in the text like this: "Click on **return** to see a listing of the available shell commands and their options."

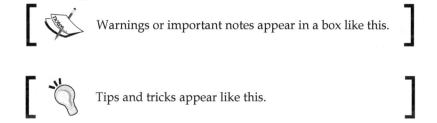

> Warnings or important notes appear in a box like this.

> Tips and tricks appear like this.

Reader feedback

Feedback from our readers is always welcome. Let us know what you think about this book—what you liked or may have disliked. Reader feedback is important for us to develop titles that you really get the most out of.

To send us general feedback, simply send an e-mail to feedback@packtpub.com, and mention the book title via the subject of your message.

If there is a topic that you have expertise in and you are interested in either writing or contributing to a book, see our author guide on www.packtpub.com/authors.

Customer support

Now that you are the proud owner of a Packt book, we have a number of things to help you to get the most from your purchase.

Downloading the example code

You can download the example code files for all Packt books you have purchased from your account at `http://www.packtpub.com`. If you purchased this book elsewhere, you can visit `http://www.packtpub.com/support` and register to have the files e-mailed directly to you.

Errata

Although we have taken every care to ensure the accuracy of our content, mistakes do happen. If you find a mistake in one of our books — maybe a mistake in the text or the code — we would be grateful if you would report this to us. By doing so, you can save other readers from frustration and help us improve subsequent versions of this book. If you find any errata, please report them by visiting `http://www.packtpub.com/submit-errata`, selecting your book, clicking on the **errata submission form** link, and entering the details of your errata. Once your errata are verified, your submission will be accepted and the errata will be uploaded on our website, or added to any list of existing errata, under the Errata section of that title.

To view the previously submitted errata, go to `https://www.packtpub.com/books/content/support` and enter the name of the book in the search field. The required information will appear under the **Errata** section.

Piracy

Piracy of copyright material on the Internet is an ongoing problem across all media. At Packt, we take the protection of our copyright and licenses very seriously. If you come across any illegal copies of our works, in any form, on the Internet, please provide us with the location address or website name immediately so that we can pursue a remedy.

Please contact us at `copyright@packtpub.com` with a link to the suspected pirated material.

We appreciate your help in protecting our authors, and our ability to bring you valuable content.

Questions

You can contact us at `questions@packtpub.com` if you are having a problem with any aspect of the book, and we will do our best to address it.

1
Introducing HBase

A **relational database management system (RDBMS)** is the right choice for most of the **online transactional processing (OLTP)** applications, and it also supports most of the **online analytical processing (OLAP)** systems. Large OLAP systems usually run very large queries that scan a wide set of records or an entire dataset containing billions of records (terabytes or petabytes in size) and face scaling issues. To address scaling issues using RDBMS, a huge investment becomes another point of concern.

The world of Big Data

Since the last decade, the amount of data being created is more than 20 terabytes per second and this size is only increasing. Not only volume and velocity but this data is also of a different variety, that is, structured and semi structured in nature, which means that data might be coming from blog posts, tweets, social network interactions, photos, videos, continuously generated log messages about what users are doing, and so on. Hence, Big Data is a combination of transactional data and interactive data. This large set of data is further used by organizations for decision making. Storing, analyzing, and summarizing these large datasets efficiently and cost effectively have become among the biggest challenges for these organizations.

In 2003, Google published a paper on the scalable distributed filesystem titled Google File System (GFS), which uses a cluster of commodity hardware to store huge amounts of data and ensure high availability by using the replication of data between nodes. Later, Google published an additional paper on processing large, distributed datasets using **MapReduce (MR)**.

For processing Big Data, platforms such as Hadoop, which inherits the basics from both GFS and MR, were developed and contributed to the community. A Hadoop-based platform is able to store and process continuously growing data in terabytes or petabytes.

The Apache Hadoop software library is a framework that allows the distributed processing of large datasets across clusters of computers.

However, Hadoop is designed to process data in the batch mode and the ability to access data randomly and near real time is completely missing. In Hadoop, processing smaller files has a larger overhead compared to big files and thus is a bad choice for low latency queries.

Later, a database solution called NoSQL evolved with multiple flavors, such as a key-value store, document-based store, column-based store, and graph-based store. NoSQL databases are suitable for different business requirements. Not only do these different flavors address scalability and availability but also take care of highly efficient read/write with data growing infinitely or, in short, Big Data.

 The NoSQL database provides a fail-safe mechanism for the storage and retrieval of data that is modeled in it, somewhat different from the tabular relations used in many relational databases.

The origin of HBase

Looking at the limitations of GFS and MR, Google approached another solution, which not only uses GFS for data storage but it is also used for processing the smaller data files very efficiently. They called this new solution BigTable.

 BigTable is a distributed storage system for managing structured data that is designed to scale to a very large size: petabytes of data across thousands of commodity servers.

Welcome to the world of HBase, http://hbase.apache.org/. HBase is a NoSQL database that primarily works on top of Hadoop. HBase is based on the storage architecture followed by the BigTable. HBase inherits the storage design from the column-oriented databases and the data access design from the keyvalue store databases where a key-based access to a specific cell of data is provided.

 In column-oriented databases, data grouped by columns and column values is stored contiguously on a disk. Such a design is highly I/O effective when dealing with very large data sets used for analytical queries where not all the columns are needed.

HBase can be defined as a sparse, distributed, persistent, multidimensional sorted map, which is indexed by a row key, column key, and timestamp. HBase is designed to run on a cluster of commodity hardware and stores both structured and semi-structured data. HBase has the ability to scale horizontally as you add more machines to the cluster.

Use cases of HBase

There are a number of use cases where HBase can be a storage system. This section discusses a few of the popular use cases for HBase and the well-known companies that have adopted HBase. Let's discuss the use cases first:

- **Handling content**: In today's world, a variety of content is available for the users for consumption. Also, the variety of application clients, such as browser, mobile, and so on, leads to an additional requirement where each client needs the same content in different formats. Users not only consume content but also generate a variety of content in a large volume with a high velocity, such as tweets, Facebook posts, images, bloging, and many more. HBase is the perfect choice as the backend of such applications, for example, many scalable content management solutions are using HBase as their backend.

- **Handling incremental data**: In many use cases, trickled data is added to a data store for further usage, such as analytics, processing, and serving. This trickled data could be coming from an advertisement's impressions such as clickstreams and user interaction data or it can be time series data. HBase is used for storage in all such cases. For example, **Open Time Series Database (OpenTSDB)** uses HBase for data storage and metrics generation. The counters feature (discussed in *Chapter 5*, *The HBase Advanced API*) is used by Facebook for counting and storing the "likes" for a particular page/image/post.

Some of the companies that are using HBase in their respective use cases are as follows:

- **Facebook** (www.facebook.com): Facebook is using HBase to power its message infrastructure. Facebook opted for HBase to scale from their old messages infrastructure which handled over 350 million users, sending over 15 billion person-to-person messages per month. HBase was selected due to the excellent scalability and performance for big workloads, along with autoload balancing and failover features and so on. Facebook also uses HBase for counting and storing the "likes" contributed by users.

- **Meetup** (www.meetup.com): Meetup uses HBase to power a site-wide, real-time activity feed system for all of its members and groups. In its architecture, group activity is written directly to HBase and indexed per member, with the member's custom feed served directly from HBase for incoming requests.

- **Twitter** (www.twitter.com): Twitter uses HBase to provide a distributed, read/write backup of all the transactional tables in Twitter's production backend. Later, this backup is used to run MapReduce jobs over the data. Additionally, its operations team uses HBase as a time series database for cluster-wide monitoring / performance data.

- **Yahoo** (www.yahoo.com): Yahoo uses HBase to store document fingerprints for detecting near-duplications. With millions of rows in the HBase table, Yahoo runs a query for finding duplicated documents with real-time traffic.

 The source for the preceding mentioned information is http://wiki.apache.org/hadoop/Hbase/PoweredBy.

Installing HBase

HBase is an Apache project and the current Version, 0.98.7, of HBase is available as a stable release. HBase Version 0.98.7 supersedes Version 0.94.x and 0.96.x.

 This book only focuses on **HBase Version 0.98.7**, as this version is fully supported and tested with Hadoop Versions 2.x and deprecates the use of Hadoop 1.x.

Hadoop 2.x is much faster compared to Hadoop 1.x and includes important bug fixes that will improve the overall HBase performance.

Older versions, 0.96.x, of HBase which are now extinct, supported both versions of Hadoop (1.x and 2.x). The HBase version prior to 0.96.x only supported Hadoop 1.x.

HBase is written in Java, works on top of Hadoop, and relies on ZooKeeper. A HBase cluster can be set up in either local or distributed mode. Distributed mode can further be classified into either pseudo-distributed or fully distributed mode.

HBase is designed and developed to work on kernel-based operating systems; hence, the commands referred to in this book are only for a kernel-based OS, for example, CentOS. In the case of Windows, it is recommended that you have a CentOS-based virtual machine to play with HBase.

An HBase cluster requires only Oracle Java to be installed on all the machines that are part of the cluster. In case any other flavor of Java, such as OpenJDK, is installed with the operating system, it needs to be uninstalled first before installing Oracle Java. HBase and other components such as Hadoop and ZooKeeper require a minimum of Java 6 or later.

Installing Java 1.7

Perform the following steps for installing Java 1.7 or later:

1. Download the `jdk-7u55-linux-x64.rpm` kit from Oracle's website at `http://www.oracle.com/technetwork/java/javase/downloads/index.html`.

2. Make sure that the file has all the permissions before installation for the root user using the following command:

   ```
   [root@localhost opt]#chmod +x jdk-7u55-linux-x64.rpm
   ```

3. Install RPM using the following command:

   ```
   [root@localhost opt]#rpm -ivh jdk-7u55-linux-x64.rpm
   ```

4. Finally, add the environment variable, `JAVA_HOME`. The following command will write the `JAVA_HOME` environment variable to the `/etc/profile` file, which contains a system-wide environment configuration:

   ```
   [root@localhost opt]# echo "export JAVA_HOME=/usr/java/
   jdk1.7.0_55" >> /etc/profile
   ```

5. Once `JAVA_HOME` is added to the profile, either close the command window and reopen it or run the following command. This step is required to reload the latest profile setting for the user:

   ```
   [root@localhost opt]# source /etc/profile
   ```

 Downloading the example code

You can download the example code files for all Packt books you have purchased from your account at http://www.packtpub.com . If you purchased this book elsewhere, you can visit http://www.packtpub.com/support and register to have the files e-mailed directly to you.

The local mode

The local or standalone mode means running all HBase services in just one Java process. Setting up HBase in the local mode is the easiest way to get started with HBase and can be used to explore further or for local development. The only step required is to download the recent release of HBase and unpack the archive (.tar) in some directory such as /opt. Perform the following steps to set up HBase in the local mode:

1. Create the hbase directory using the following commands:

   ```
   [root@localhost opt]# mkdir myhbase

   [root@localhost opt]# cd myhbase
   ```

2. Download the hbase binaries as the archive (.tar) files and unpack it, as shown in the following command:

   ```
   [root@localhost myhbase]# wget http://mirrors.sonic.net/apache/
   hbase/stable/hbase-0.98.7-hadoop2-bin.tar.gz
   ```

   In the preceding command, http://mirrors.sonic.net/apache/hbase/ can be different for different users, which is based on the user's location. Check the suggested mirror site at http://www.apache.org/dyn/closer. cgi/hbase/ for the new URL.

    HBase version 0.98.7 is available for Hadoop 1 and 2 as hbase-0.98.7-hadoop1-bin.tar.gz and hbase-0.98.7-hadoop2-bin.tar.gz. It is recommended that you use Hadoop 2 only with HBase 0.98.7, and Hadoop 1 is available as a deprecated support. In the local mode, a Hadoop cluster is not required as it can use the Hadoop binaries provided in the lib directory of HBase. Other versions of HBase can also be checked out at http://www.apache.org/dyn/closer.cgi/hbase/.

3. Once the HBase binaries are downloaded, extract them using the following command:

   ```
   [root@localhost myhbase]# tar xvfz hbase-0.98.7-hadoop2-bin.tar.gz
   ```

4. Add the environment variable, HBASE_HOME. The following command will write the HBASE_HOME environment variable to the /etc/profile file, which contains system-wide environment configuration:

   ```
   [root@localhost myhbase]# echo "export HBASE_HOME=/opt/myhbase/
   hbase-0.98.7-hadoop2" >> /etc/profile
   ```

5. Once HBASE_HOME is added to the profile, either close the command window and reopen it or run the following command; this step is required to reload the latest profile settings for the user:

```
[root@localhost opt]# source /etc/profile
```

6. Edit the configuration file, conf/hbase-site.xml, and set the data directory for HBase by assigning a value to the property key named hbase.rootdir and hbase.zookeeper.property.dataDir, as follows:

```
<property>
  <name>hbase.rootdir</name>
  <value>file:///opt/myhbase/datadirectory</value>
</property>
<property>
    <name>hbase.zookeeper.property.dataDir</name>
    <value>/opt/myhbase/zookeeper</value>
</property>
```

The default base directory value for the hbase.rootdir and hbase.zookeeper.property.dataDir properties is /tmp/hbase-${user.name}, that is, /tmp/hbase-root for the "root" user which may lead to the possibility of data loss at the time of server reboot. Hence, it is always advisable to set the value for this property to avoid a data-loss scenario.

7. Start HBase and verify the output with the following command:

```
[root@localhost opt]# cd /opt/myhbase/hbase-0.98.7-hadoop2
[root@localhost hbase-0.98.7-hadoop2]# bin/start-hbase.sh
```

This gives the following output:

```
[root@localhost hbase-0.98.7-hadoop2]# bin/start-hbase.sh
starting master, logging to /opt/myhbase/hbase-0.98.7-hadoop2/logs
/hbase-root-master-localhost.localdomain.out
[root@localhost hbase-0.98.7-hadoop2]#
```

HBase also comes with a preinstalled web-based management console that can be accessed using `http://localhost:60010`. By default, it is deployed on HBase's Master host at port `60010`. This UI provides information about various components such as region servers, tables, running tasks, logs, and so on, as shown in the following screenshot:

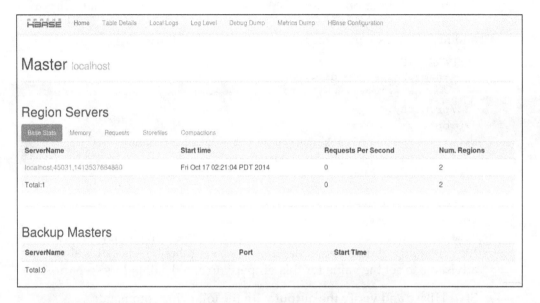

The HBase tables and monitored tasks are shown in the following screenshot:

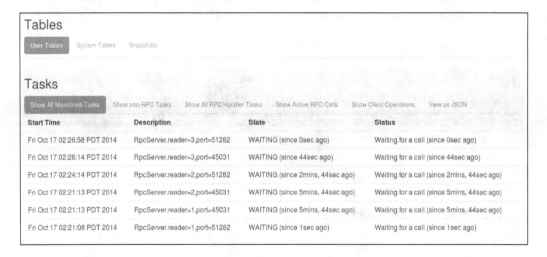

The following screenshot displays information about the HBase attributes, provided by the UI:

Software Attributes

Attribute Name	Value	Description
HBase Version	0.98.7-hadoop2, r800c23e2207aa3f9bddb7e9514d8340bcfb89277	HBase version and revision
HBase Compiled	Wed Oct 8 15:58:11 PDT 2014, apurtell	When HBase version was compiled and by whom
Hadoop Version	2.2.0, r1529768	Hadoop version and revision
Hadoop Compiled	2013-10-07T06:28Z, hortonmu	When Hadoop version was compiled and by whom
Zookeeper Quorum	localhost:2181	Addresses of all registered ZK servers. For more, see zk dump.
HBase Root Directory	file:/opt/myhbase/datadirectory	Location of HBase home directory
HMaster Start Time	Fri Oct 17 02:21:06 PDT 2014	Date stamp of when this HMaster was started
HMaster Active Time	Fri Oct 17 02:21:06 PDT 2014	Date stamp of when this HMaster became active
HBase Cluster ID	5e0a6890-7e44-4205-ae6f-9208abc3e58a	Unique identifier generated for each HBase cluster
Load average	2.00	Average number of regions per regionserver. Naive computation.
Coprocessors	[]	Coprocessors currently loaded by the master

Once the HBase setup is done correctly, the following directories are created in a local filesystem, as shown in the following screenshot:

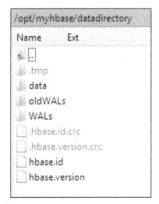

The pseudo-distributed mode

The standalone/local mode is only useful for basic operations and is not at all suitable for real-world workloads. In the pseudo-distributed mode, all HBase services (HMaster, HRegionServer, and Zookeeper) run as separate Java processes on a single machine. This mode can be useful during the testing phase.

In the pseudo-distributed mode, HDFS setup is another prerequisite (HDFS setup also needs to be present in pseudo-distributed mode). After setting up Hadoop and downloading the HBase binary, edit the `conf/hbase-site.xml` configuration file. Also, set the HBase in the running mode by assigning a value to the property key named `hbase.cluster.distributed`, as well as the data storage pointer to the running Hadoop HDFS instance by assigning a value to the property key named `hbase.rootdir`:

```
<property>
      <name>hbase.cluster.distributed</name>
      <value>true</value>
</property>

<property>
    <name>hbase.rootdir</name>
<value>hdfs://localhost:9000/hbase</value>
</property>
```

Once the settings are done, we can use the following command to start HBase:

```
[root@localhost opt]# cd /opt/myhbase/hbase-0.96.2-hadoop2
[root@localhost hbase-0.96.2-hadoop2]# bin/start-hbase.sh
```

 Before starting HBase, make sure that the Hadoop services are running and working fine.

Once HBase is configured correctly, the `jps` command should show the HMaster and HRegionServer processes running along with the Hadoop processes. Use the `hadoop fs` command in Hadoop's `bin/` directory to list the directories created in HDFS as follows:

```
[root@localhost opt]# hadoop fs -ls /hbase
Found 7 items
drwxr-xr-x    - hbase users         0 2014-10-20 14:28 /hbase/.tmp
drwxr-xr-x    - hbase users         0 2014-10-20 17:29 /hbase/WALs
```

```
drwxr-xr-x    - hbase users         0 2014-10-20 14:38 /hbase/corrupt
drwxr-xr-x    - hbase users         0 2014-10-20 14:28 /hbase/data
-rw-r--r--    3 hbase users        42 2014-10-20 14:21 /hbase/hbase.id
-rw-r--r--    3 hbase users         7 2014-10-20 14:21 /hbase/hbase.
version
drwxr-xr-x    - hbase users         0 2014-10-20 27:29 /hbase/oldWALs
```

The fully distributed mode

A pseudo-distributed mode, where all the HBase services (HMaster, HRegionServer, and Zookeeper) run as separate Java processes on a single machine, is preferred for a local development environment or test environment. However, for a production environment, fully distributed mode is a must. In the fully distributed mode, an HBase cluster is set up on multiple nodes and HBase services run on these different cluster nodes. To enable fully distributed mode, add the `hbase.cluster.distributed` property to `conf/hbase-site.xml` and set it to `true`; also point the `hbase.rootdir` HBase to the HDFS node:

```
<property>
    <name>hbase.rootdir</name>
    <value>hdfs://<HDFSNameNodeHost>:9000/hbase</value>
</property>
<property>
    <name>hbase.cluster.distributed</name>
    <value>true<value>
</property>
```

> This book does not touch upon information on building a fully distributed HBase cluster and also does not talk about the hardware considerations, such as, server configurations, network settings, and so on; and software considerations, such as server OS setting, Hadoop settings, and so on. For this book, it is recommended that you use either the local mode or the pseudo-distributed mode.

For understanding this mode in depth, the building blocks that play a vital role in a fully distributed HBase cluster need to be understood well. The next section will give you a glimpse of what these components are.

Understanding HBase cluster components

In fully distributed and pseudo-distributed modes, a HBase cluster has many components such as HBase Master, ZooKeeper, RegionServers, HDFS DataNodes, and so on, discussed as follows:

- **HBase Master**: HBase Master coordinates the HBase cluster and is responsible for administrative operations. It is a lightweight process that does not require too many hardware resources. A large cluster might have multiple HBase Master components to avoid cases that have a single point of failure. In this highly available cluster with multiple HBase Master components, only once HBase Master is active and the rest of HBase Master servers get in sync with the active server asynchronously. Selection of the next HBase Master in case of failover is done with the help of the ZooKeeper ensemble.

- **ZooKeeper**: ZooKeeper is a centralized service for maintaining configuration information, naming, providing distributed synchronization, and providing group services. Similar to HBase Master, ZooKeeper is again a lightweight process. By default, a ZooKeeper process is started and stopped by HBase but it can be managed separately as well. The HBASE_MANAGES_ZK variable in conf/hbase-env.sh with the default value true signifies that HBase is going to manage ZooKeeper. We can specify the ZooKeeper configuration in the native zoo.cfg file or its values such as client, port, and so on directly in conf/hbase-site.xml. It is advisable that you have an odd number of ZooKeeper ensembles such as one/three/five for more host failure tolerance. The following is an example of hbase-site.xml with ZooKeeper settings:

```
<property>
    <name>hbase.zookeeper.property.clientPort</name>
    <value>2222</value>
</property>
<property>
    <name>hbase.zookeeper.quorum</name>
    <value>ZooKeeperhost1, ZooKeeperhost2, ZooKeeperhost3<value>
</property>
<property>
    <name>hbase.zookeeper.property.dataDir</name>
    <value>/opt/zookeeper<value>
</property>
```

- **RegionServers**: In HBase, horizontal scalability is defined with a term called region. Regions are nothing but a sorted range of rows stored continuously. In HBase architecture, a set of regions is stored on the region server. By default, the region server runs on port 60030. In an HBase cluster based on HDFS, Hadoop DataNodes and RegionServers are typically called slave nodes as they are both responsible for server data and are usually collocated in the cluster. A list of the region servers is specified in the `conf/regionservers` file with each region server on a separate line, and the start/stop of these region servers is controlled by the script files responsible for an HBase cluster's start/stop.

- **HBase data storage system**: HBase is developed using pluggable architecture; hence, for the data storage layer, HBase is not tied with HDFS. Rather, it can also be plugged in with other file storage systems such as the local filesystem (primarily used in standalone mode), S3 (Amazon's Simple Storage Service), CloudStore (also known as Kosmos filesystem) or a self-developed filesystem.

Apart from the mentioned components, there are other considerations as well, such as hardware and software considerations, that are not within the scope of this book.

> The backup HBase Master server and the additional region servers can be started in the pseudo-distributed mode using the utility provided bin directory as follows:
>
> ```
> [root@localhost hbase-0.96.2-hadoop2]# bin/local-
> master-backup.sh 2 3
> ```
>
> The preceding command will start the two additional HBase Master backup servers on the same box. Each HMaster server uses three ports (`16010`, `16020`, and `16030` by default) and the new backup servers will be using ports `16012/16022/16032` and `16013/16023/16033`.
>
> ```
> [root@localhost hbase-0.96.2-hadoop2]# bin/local-
> regionservers.sh start 2 3
> ```
>
> The preceding command will start the two additional HBase region servers on the same box using ports `16202/16302`.

Start playing

Now that we have everything installed and running, let's start playing with it and try out a few commands to get a feel of HBase. HBase comes with a command-line interface that works for both local and distributed modes. The HBase shell is developed in JRuby and can run in both interactive (recommended for simple commands) and batch modes (recommended for running shell script programs). Let's start the HBase shell in the interactive mode as follows:

```
[root@localhost hbase-0.98.7-hadoop2]# bin/hbase shell
```

The preceding command gives the following output:

```
[root@localhost hbase-0.98.7-hadoop2]# bin/hbase shell
2014-10-20 02:33:00,531 INFO  [main] Configuration.deprecation: hadoop.native.
lib is deprecated. Instead, use io.native.lib.available
HBase Shell; enter 'help<RETURN>' for list of supported commands.
Type "exit<RETURN>" to leave the HBase Shell
Version 0.98.7-hadoop2, r800c23e2207aa3f9bddb7e9514d8340bcfb89277, Wed Oct  8
15:58:11 PDT 2014

hbase(main):001:0>
```

Type `help` and click on **return** to see a listing of the available shell commands and their options. Remember that all the commands are case-sensitive.

The following is a list of some simple commands to get your hands dirty with HBase:

- `status`: This verifies whether HBase is up and running, as shown in the following screenshot:

```
hbase(main):004:0> status
1 servers, 0 dead, 2.0000 average load
```

- `create '<table_name>', '<column_family_name>'`: This creates a table with one column family. We can use multiple column family names as well, as shown in the following screenshot:

```
hbase(main):003:0> create 'tab1', 'cf1'
0 row(s) in 0.4090 seconds

=> Hbase::Table - tab1
hbase(main):004:0> create 'tab2', 'cf1', 'cf2'
0 row(s) in 0.1700 seconds

=> Hbase::Table - tab2
```

- `list`: This provides the list of tables, as shown in the following screenshot:

```
hbase(main):005:0> list
TABLE
tab1
tab2
2 row(s) in 0.0510 seconds

=> ["tab1", "tab2"]
hbase(main):006:0>
```

- `put '<table_name>', '<row_num>', 'column_family:key', 'value'`:
  This command is used to put data in the table in a column family manner,
  as shown in the following screenshot. HBase is a schema-less database and
  provides the flexibility to store any type of data without defining it:

```
hbase(main):006:0> put 'tab1', 'row-1', 'cf1:greet', 'Hello'
0 row(s) in 0.1250 seconds

hbase(main):007:0> put 'tab1', 'row-1', 'cf1:pie', 3.14
0 row(s) in 0.0260 seconds

hbase(main):008:0> put 'tab1', 'row-2', 'cf1:pie', 3.14
0 row(s) in 0.0120 seconds
```

- `get '<table_name>', '<row_num>'`: This command is used to read a
  particular row from the table, as shown in the following screenshot:

```
hbase(main):009:0> get 'tab1', 'row-1'
COLUMN                 CELL
 cf1:greet                timestamp=1413798501568, value=Hello
 cf1:pie                  timestamp=1413798526740, value=3.14
2 row(s) in 0.0380 seconds

hbase(main):010:0> get 'tab1', 'row-2'
COLUMN                 CELL
 cf1:pie                  timestamp=1413798651419, value=3.14
1 row(s) in 0.0090 seconds

hbase(main):011:0>
```

- `scan '<table_name >'`: This scans the complete table and outputs the
  results, as shown in the following screenshot:

```
hbase(main):011:0> scan 'tab1'
ROW                   COLUMN+CELL
 row-1                    column=cf1:greet, timestamp=1413798501568, value=Hello
 row-1                    column=cf1:pie, timestamp=1413798526740, value=3.14
 row-2                    column=cf1:pie, timestamp=1413798651419, value=3.14
2 row(s) in 0.0510 seconds

hbase(main):012:0>
```

- `delete '<table_name>', '<row_num>', 'column_family:key'`: This deletes the specified value, as shown in the following screenshot:

```
hbase(main):012:0> delete 'tab1', 'row-1', 'cf1:pie'
0 row(s) in 0.0440 seconds

hbase(main):013:0> scan 'tab1'
ROW                  COLUMN+CELL
 row-1               column=cf1:greet, timestamp=1413798501568, value=Hello
 row-2               column=cf1:pie, timestamp=1413798651419, value=3.14
2 row(s) in 0.0150 seconds

hbase(main):014:0> █
```

- `describe '<table_name>'`: This describes the metadata information about the table, as shown in the following screenshot:

```
hbase(main):014:0> describe 'tab1'
DESCRIPTION                                             ENABLED
 'tab1', {NAME => 'cf1', DATA_BLOCK_ENCODING => 'N true
 ONE', BLOOMFILTER => 'ROW', REPLICATION_SCOPE =>
 '0', VERSIONS => '1', COMPRESSION => 'NONE', MIN_
 VERSIONS => '0', TTL => 'FOREVER', KEEP_DELETED_C
 ELLS => 'false', BLOCKSIZE => '65536', IN_MEMORY
 => 'false', BLOCKCACHE => 'true'}
1 row(s) in 0.0850 seconds

hbase(main):015:0> █
```

- `drop '<table_name>'`: This command will drop the table. However, before executing this command, we should first execute `disable '<tablename>'`, as shown in the following screenshot:

```
hbase(main):015:0> disable 'tab1'
0 row(s) in 1.4800 seconds

hbase(main):016:0> drop 'tab1'
0 row(s) in 0.1940 seconds

hbase(main):017:0> list
TABLE
tab2
1 row(s) in 0.0470 seconds

=> ["tab2"]
hbase(main):018:0> █
```

- Finally, exit the shell and stop using HBase, as shown in the following screenshot:

```
hbase(main):018:0> exit
[root@localhost hbase-0.98.7-hadoop2]# bin/stop-hbase.sh
stopping hbase......................
[root@localhost hbase-0.98.7-hadoop2]# █
```

 Refer to the following link for more commands: `http://wiki.apache.org/hadoop/Hbase/Shell`

Summary

In this chapter, we started our journey by understanding what the NoSQL world is and then got introduced to HBase. We also learned how to install Apache HBase 0.98.7 and also set up an HBase cluster in different possible modes. Finally, we tried a few commands using the HBase command-line interface HBase shell. In the next chapter, we will take a look at the key concepts of HBase.

2
Defining the Schema

In this chapter, we are going to learn some of the basic concepts of the column family database, that is, HBase, and cover the following topics:

- Data modeling
- Designing tables
- CRUD operations

Let's dive in and start off by taking a look at how we can model data in HBase.

Data modeling in HBase

In the RDBMS world, data modeling has principles around tables, columns, data types, size, and so on, and the only supported format is structured data. HBase is quite different in this aspect, as in each row, it can store different numbers of columns and data types, making it ideal for storing so-called semi-structured data. Storing semi-structured data not only impacts the physical schema but also the logical schema of HBase. For the same reason, some features such as relational constraints are also not present in HBase.

Similar to a typical RDBMS, tables are composed of rows and these rows are composed of columns. Rows in HBase are identified by a unique rowkey and are compared with each other at the byte level, which resembles a primary key in RDBMS.

In HBase, columns are organized into column families. There is no restriction on the number of columns that can be grouped together in a single column family. This column family is part of the data definition statement used to create the HBase table.

At the storage level, all columns in a column family are stored in a single file, called HFile, as key-value pairs in the binary format. These HFiles are ordered immutable maps which are internally represented as data blocks with a block index.

In HBase, the placeholder for the column value is called cell. Each cell stores the most recent value and the historical values for the column. These values are placed in a descending order on the timestamp and ensure a faster read performance.

Each value contained within a cell in the table can be represented by a combination of the rowkey, column family, column key, and timestamp. The following image of a table shows the organization of values in the table:

Row Keys	Column Family :: Customer		
	Name	email	Phone
ROW 1 Cell	David Cell	david@gmail.com Cell	982 765 2345 Cell
ROW 2 Cell	John Cell	john@rediff.com Cell	763 456 1234 Cell
ROW 3 Cell	Elan Cell	elan@hotmail.com Cell	554 123 0987 Cell
ROW 4 Cell	Maria Cell	maria@test.net Cell	763 451 4587 Cell 863 341 4123

Each Cell may have multiple version of data Distinguished by time stamp

Like column families that group columns, HBase has a concept called regions, where it groups the continuous range of rows and stores them together at lower levels in region servers. Regions can also be thought of as data partitions in the RDBMS world and help to achieve scalability in the overall HBase architecture. A maximum size is defined for regions, and once the limit is exceeded, the region is split into two from the middle. This process is synonymous to auto-sharding in the RDBMS world.

In HBase, records are stored in HFiles as key-value pairs, and this HFile is, in turn, stored as a binary file. Records from a single column family might be split across multiple HFiles, but a single HFile cannot contain data for multiple column families.

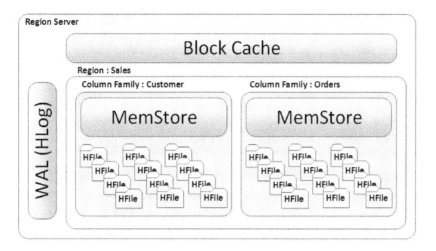

The preceding diagram shows how different data storage level components are organized. The **region server** contains the region **sales**, having two column families, **customer** and **orders**. Each column family has an in-memory storage, and single column family records might have been written to multiple HFiles. In HBase, the region server is treated as a datanode and supports multiple regions (represents tables here). When data is written, by default, it goes to the **write ahead log** (**WAL**) and the MemStore. HFile is created once the data present in the MemStore is flushed to the disk and in case of flush failure, data is retrieved from WAL (we will discuss all these components in detail in *Chapter 4, The HBase Architecture*).

Designing tables

In HBase, when modeling the schema for any table, a designer should also keep in mind the following, among other things:

- The number of column families and which data goes to which column family
- The maximum number of columns in each column family
- The type of data to be stored in the column
- The number of historical values that need to be maintained for each column
- The structure of a rowkey

Once we have answers, certain practices are followed to ensure optimal table design. Some of the design practices are as follows:

- Data for a given column family goes into a single store on HDFS. This store might consist of multiple HFiles, which eventually get converted to a single HFile using compaction techniques.

- Columns in a column family are also stored together on the disk, and the columns with different access patterns should be kept in different column families.

- If we design tables with fewer columns and many rows (a tall table), we might achieve O(1) operations but also compromise with atomicity.

- Access patterns should be completed in a single API call. Multiple calls are not a good sign of design.

We not only need to design the table schema to store data in a column-family layout but also consider the read/write pattern for the table, that is, how the application is going to access the data from an HBase table. Similarly, rowkeys should be designed based on the access patterns, as regions represent a range of rows based on the rowkeys and the HFiles store the rows sorted on the disk. Hence, the rowkey is a crucial element to the performance of I/O interactions with HBase.

 HBase doesn't support cross-row transactions, so the client code should avoid any kind of transactional logic to support simplicity.

HBase drives the design from BigTable of Google as one-row-per-account which might easily hold multiple terabytes in a single row with no problems or with a poor design. However, the same information can also be stored in a tall table (lots of rows with fewer columns), which also provide performance benefits. This performance benefit also comes with a cost of atomicity. The physical storage for both the table designs is essentially the same.

Accessing HBase

In the previous chapter, we saw how to create a table and simple data operations using the HBase shell. HBase can be accessed using a variety of clients, such as REST clients, Thrift client, object mapper framework—Kundera, and so on. HBase clients are discussed in detail in *Chapter 6, HBase Clients*. HBase also offers advanced Java-based APIs for playing with tables and column families. (HBase shell is a wrapper around this Java API.) This API also supports metadata management, for example, data compression for column family, region split, and so on. In addition to schema definition, the API also provides an interface for a table scan with various functions such as limiting the number of columns returned or limiting the number of versions of each cell to be stored. For data manipulation, the Hbase API supports create, read, update, and delete operations on individual rows. This API comes with many advanced features, which will be discussed throughout this book.

> In most parts of the book, all of the sample code or full examples will be using Java-based HBase API only. There are many other options layered on top of the Java API to access HBase, that is, ORM—Kundera, REST gateway, Phoenix, and so on. These clients are covered in *Chapter 6, HBase Clients*, in detail.

Establishing a connection

Before performing any kind of operation in an HBase table using Java-based HBase API, a connection needs to be established with the help of the HConnection class. This class is managed by the shared HConnectionManager class. Once the connection is established, it returns an HTable instance located in the org.apache.hadoop. hbase.client package. This class provides the user with all the functionality needed to store and retrieve data:

```
HTableInterface usersTable = new HTable("Costumers");
```

From the preceding code, we can verify that the usage of the HConnection and HConnectionManager classes is not mandatory as the HTable constructor reads the default configuration to create a connection. If there is a need to use or define the connection explicitly, the following code can be used with a custom configuration:

```
Configuration newConfig = new Configuration(defaultConfig);
HConnection connection =
  HConnectionManager.createConnection(newConfig);
HTableInterface table = connection.getTable("Costumers");
```

The HTable class is not thread-safe as concurrent modifications are not safe. Hence, a single instance of HTable for each thread should be used in any application. For multiple HTable instances with the same configuration reference, the same underlying HConnection instance can be used.

Creating HTable instances also comes at a cost. Creating an HTable instance is a slow process as the creation of each HTable instance involves the scanning of the .META table to check whether the table actually exists, which makes the operation very costly. Hence, it is not recommended that you use a new HTable instance for each request where the number of concurrent requests are very high.

Whenever there is a requirement of multiple instances of HTable, consider using the HTablePool class. The following constructor can be used to create an instance of HTablePool:

```
HTablePool()
HTablePool(Configuration config, int maxSize)
HTablePool(Configuration config, int maxSize,
HTableInterfaceFactory tableFactory)
```

The HTablePool class creates a pool with the HTable class instances with the configuration object, and setting the maxSize parameter defining the HTable instances to count a pool. Here is the code for getting the HTable instance from HTablePool:

```
HTableInterface usersTable = pool.getTable("Costumers");
```

CRUD operations

A rowkey primarily represents each row uniquely in the HBase table, whereas other keys such as column family, timestamp, and so on are used to locate a piece of data in an HBase table. The HBase API provides the following methods to support the CRUD operations:

- Put
- Get
- Delete
- Scan
- Increment

Let's discuss the first three methods in detail and the rest will be covered in the coming chapters.

Writing data

In HBase, when a write request is received, by default, the data is synchronously written into HLog, also referred to as the write ahead log or commit log and to the memstore. Writing data at two places ensures data durability. The memstore is a write buffer that accumulates the data before committing it to the disk permanently in the form of an HFile. Every time the memstore flushes the data to the disk, a new HFile is created. In case of an HBase cluster failure, data that is not committed to an HFile from the memstore, the write buffer is recovered from the HLog file present in the filesystem. This way of writing to HBase is applicable to both row creation and updation.

A `Put` class instance is used to store data in an HBase table. For storing data in a table, create a `Put` instance with `rowkey` using any of the constructors, as follows:

```
Put(byte[] rowkey)
Put(byte[] rowArray, int rowOffset, int rowLength)
Put(byte[] rowkey, long ts)
Put(byte[] rowArray, int rowOffset, int rowLength, long ts)
Put p = new Put (Bytes.toBytes("John"));
```

HBase stores all the data, including the rowkey, in the form of a byte array and a Java utility class, bytes define various static utility methods for converting Java data types to and from a byte.

Once a `Put` instance is created using the `rowkey` component, the next step is to add the data by using either of the following method definitions:

```
add(byte[] family, byte[] qualifier, byte[] value)
add(byte[] family, byte[] qualifier, long ts, byte[] value)
add (byte[] family, ByteBuffer qualifier, long ts, ByteBuffer value)
add (Cell kv)
```

The `add()` option takes a column family along with an optional timestamp or one single cell as a parameter. In case the timestamp is not defined, the region server sets it for the data inserted. Here is a complete example of how to write data to HBase:

```
import java.io.IOException;

import org.apache.hadoop.conf.Configuration;
import org.apache.hadoop.hbase.HBaseConfiguration;
import org.apache.hadoop.hbase.client.HTable;
```

```
import org.apache.hadoop.hbase.client.Put;
import org.apache.hadoop.hbase.util.Bytes;

public class SinglePutEx {
public static void main(String[] args) throws IOException {
  // Get instance of Default Configuration
  Configuration conf = HBaseConfiguration.create();

// Get table instance
HTable table = new HTable(conf, "tab1");

// Create Put with rowkey
  Put put = new Put(Bytes.toBytes("row-1"));

// Add a column with value "Hello", in "cf1:greet", to the // Put.
  put.add(Bytes.toBytes("cf1"), Bytes.toBytes("greet"),
      Bytes.toBytes("Hello"));

// Add more column with value "John", in "cf1:person",
// to the Put.
  put.add(Bytes.toBytes("cf1"), Bytes.toBytes("person"),
      Bytes.toBytes("John"));

  table.put(put);
  table.close();
}
}
```

Data can be inserted into HBase for a single row or as a batch representing multiple rows using the following method of the `HTable` class:

```
void put(List<Put> puts)
```

A list of `Put` instances can be created, as follows:

```
List<Put> puts = new ArrayList<Put>();
Put put1 = new Put(Bytes.toBytes("row-1"));
put1.add(Bytes.toBytes("cf1"), Bytes.toBytes("greet"),Bytes.
toBytes("Hello"));
puts.add(put1);
....
```

A few other important methods of the Put class can be found in the following table:

Method name	Description
`get(byte[] family, byte[] qualifier)`	This returns a list of all the key-value objects with a matching column family and a qualifier
`has(byte[] family, byte[] qualifier, byte[] value)`	This is a convenience method that determines whether the object's family map contains a value assigned to the given family, qualifier, and timestamp

Reading data

HBase uses an LRU cache for reads, which is also called the block cache. This block cache keeps the frequently accessed data from the HFiles in the memory to avoid frequent disk reads, and every column family has its own block cache. Whenever a read request arrives, the block cache is first checked for the relevant row. If it is not found, the HFiles on the disk are then checked for the same. Similar to the Put class, the Get class instance is used to read the data back from the HBase table. The HBase table defines the following method for reading the data and takes the Get class instance as an argument:

```
Result get(Get getInst)
```

This method extracts certain cells from a given row. Here, the Get class instance can be created by either of the class constructors:

```
Get(byte[] rowkey)
```

This constructor creates a Get operation for the specified row identified by the rowkey. For narrowing down the data search to a specific cell, additional methods are provided in the following table:

Method name	Description
`addFamily(byte[] family)`	Get all columns from the specified family
`addColumn(byte[] family, byte[] qualifier)`	Get the column from the specific family with the specified qualifier
`setTimeRange(long minStamp, long maxStamp)`	Get versions of columns only within the specified timestamp range (minStamp, maxStamp)
`setTimeStamp(long timestamp)`	Get versions of columns with the specified timestamp
`setMaxVersions(int max versions)`	Get up to the specified number of versions of each column. The default value of the maximum version returned is 1 which is the latest cell value.

The following is a complete example of how to read data to HBase:

```java
import java.io.IOException;

import org.apache.hadoop.conf.Configuration;
import org.apache.hadoop.hbase.HBaseConfiguration;
import org.apache.hadoop.hbase.client.Get;
import org.apache.hadoop.hbase.client.HTable;
import org.apache.hadoop.hbase.client.Result;
import org.apache.hadoop.hbase.util.Bytes;

public class SingleGetEx {
  public static void main(String[] args) throws IOException {
  // Get instance of Default Configuration
  Configuration conf = HBaseConfiguration.create();

// Get table instance
  HTable table = new HTable(conf, "tab1");

// Create Get with rowkey
  Get get = new Get(Bytes.toBytes("row-1"));

// Add a column with value "Hello", in "cf1:greet", to the // Put.
get.addColumn(Bytes.toBytes("cf1"), Bytes.toBytes("greet"));

Result result = table.get(get);
  byte[] val = result.getValue(Bytes.toBytes("cf1"),
      Bytes.toBytes("greet"));
  System.out.println("Cell Value: " + Bytes.toString(val));
  table.close();
  }
}
```

Data reading in HBase can take place for a single row or in the form of a batch representing multiple rows using the following method of the HTable class:

```java
Results[] get(List<Get> gets)
```

Here, List can be defined as follows:

```java
List<Get> gets = new ArrayList<Get>();
Get get1 = new Get(Bytes.toBytes("row-1"));
get1.add(Bytes.toBytes("cf1"), Bytes.toBytes("greet"));
gets.add(get1);
...
```

Some of the other important methods defined in the Get class are stated in the following table:

Method name	Description
getFamilyMap()	Method for retrieving the get method's family map
getMaxResultsPerColumnFamily()	Method for retrieving the get method's maximum number of values to return per column family
getCacheBlocks()	Gets whether blocks should be cached for this method

Updating data

Data updation in HBase is done in a manner that is similar to writing it. The new data is updated in the table using a Put instance. The following is the sample code for updating data in HBase:

```
// Get instance of Default Configuration
Configuration conf = HBaseConfiguration.create();

//Get table instance
HTable table = new HTable(conf, "tab1");

// Create Put with rowkey
Put put = new Put(Bytes.toBytes("row-1"));

// Update a column with value "Hello", in "cf1:greet", to the
// Put.
put.add(Bytes.toBytes("cf1"), Bytes.toBytes("greet"),
    Bytes.toBytes("GoodMorning"));

// Update more column with value "David", in "cf1:person", to the //
Put.
put.add(Bytes.toBytes("cf1"), Bytes.toBytes("person"),
    Bytes.toBytes("David"));

table.put(put);
table.close();
```

Deleting data

The `Delete` command only marks the cell for deletion rather than deleting the data immediately. The actual deletion is performed when the compaction of HFiles is done to reconcile these marked records and to free the space occupied by the deleted data.

> Compaction is the process of choosing HFiles from a region and combining them. In a major compaction process, it picks all the HFiles and writes back the key-values to the output HFile that are not marked as deleted. Whereas, in a minor compaction, it only takes a few files placed together and combines them into one. Also, minor compaction does not filter the deleted files. The compaction process takes care of the versions and uses the ExploringCompactionPolicy algorithms internally.

Similar to the `Put` and `Get` classes, the `Delete` class instance is used to delete the data from the HBase table. The HBase table defines the following method for deleting the data, which takes the `Delete` class instance as an argument:

```
void delete(Delete deleteInst)
```

This method deletes the latest cells from a given row. Here, the `Delete` class instance can be created using either of the class constructors:

```
Delete(byte[] row)
Delete(byte[] rowArray, int rowOffset, int rowLength)
Delete(byte[] rowArray, int rowOffset, int rowLength, long ts)
Delete(byte[] row, long timestamp)
Delete(Delete d)
```

This constructor creates a `Delete` operation for the specified row identified by the rowkey. For narrowing down the data search to a specific cell, additional methods provided within the `Delete` class are as follows:

Method name	Description

`deleteColumn(byte[] family, byte[] qualifier)`
 	
`deleteColumn(byte[] family, byte[] qualifier, long timestamp)`
	This deletes the latest version of the specified column based on the timestamp

`deleteColumns(byte[] family, byte[] qualifier)`	This deletes all the versions of the specified column
`deleteFamily(byte[] family)`	This deletes all the versions of all columns of the specified family

Method name	Description
deleteFamily(byte[] family, long timestamp)	This deletes all the columns of the specified family with a timestamp less than or equal to the specified timestamp
deleteFamilyVersion(byte[] family, long timestamp)	This deletes all the columns of the specified family with a timestamp equal to the specified timestamp

Here is a complete code example for deleting data from HBase:

```
import java.io.IOException;

import org.apache.hadoop.conf.Configuration;
import org.apache.hadoop.hbase.HBaseConfiguration;
import org.apache.hadoop.hbase.client.Delete;
import org.apache.hadoop.hbase.client.HTable;
import org.apache.hadoop.hbase.client.Result;
import org.apache.hadoop.hbase.util.Bytes;

public class SingleGetEx {
    public static void main(String[] args) throws IOException {
    // Get instance of Default Configuration
    Configuration conf = HBaseConfiguration.create();

    // Get table instance
    HTable table = new HTable(conf, "tab1");

    // Create Delete with rowkey
    Delete delete = new Delete(Bytes.toBytes("row-1"));

    // Add a column with value "Hello", in "cf1:greet", to the Put.
    delete.deleteColumns(Bytes.toBytes("cf1"),Bytes.toBytes("greet"));

    table.delete(delete);
    table.close();
    }
}
```

Data deletion in HBase can happen for a single row or in the form of a batch representing multiple rows using the following method of the HTable class:

```
void delete(List<Delete> deletes)
```

Here, `List` can be defined as follows:

```
List<Delete> deletes = new ArrayList<Delete>();
Delete delete1 = new Delete(Bytes.toBytes("row-1"));
delete1.deleteColumn(Bytes.toBytes("cf1"), Bytes.toBytes("greet"));
deletes.add(delete1);
...
```

Another important method defined in the `Get` class is given as follows:

Methods name	Description
`setTimestamp(long timestamp)`	This sets the timestamp of `delete`

As discussed earlier, HBase maintains versions of data for each cell; this principle is applicable to all the CRUD operations. That is, `deleteColumn(...)` deletes the specific version based on parameters, and `deleteColumns(...)` deletes all the versions for a specified cell. Similarly, the data reading process reads the version of data based on the parameter values provided.

Summary

In this chapter, we learned the basics of modeling data and some strategies to consider when designing a table in HBase. We also learned how to perform basic CRUD operations on the table created using various APIs provided by HBase. In the next chapter, we will look into HBase table keys, table scan, and some other advanced features such as filters.

3
Advanced Data Modeling

So far, we have learned the basic building blocks of HBase schema designing and the CRUD operations over the designed schema. In this chapter, we are going to dive deep and learn the advanced level concepts of HBase, covering the following topics:

- Understanding keys
- HBase table scans
- Implementing filters

Let's get an insight into the listed advanced concepts of HBase.

Understanding keys

In HBase, we primarily have the following keys to handle data within the tables:

- **Row Key**: This provides a logical representation of an entire row, containing all the column families and column qualifiers
- **Column Key**: This is formed by combining the column family and the column qualifier

Logically, the data stored in cells is arranged in a tabular format, but physically, these tabular rows are stored as linear sets of the actual cells. These linear sets of cells contain all the real data inside them.

Additionally, the data within multiple versions of the same cell is also stored as a separate linear set of cells and a timestamp is added, along with the cell data stored. These linear sets of cells are sorted in descending order by their timestamp so that the HBase client always fetches the most recent value of the cell data.

The following diagram represents how data is stored physically on the disk:

Row Keys	Column Family :: CF1		Column Family :: CF2	
	Col-1	Col-2	Col-1	Col-2
ROW-1	David	982 765 2345		
ROW-2			John	
ROW-3	Elan			909 451 4587 / 863 441 4123
ROW-4	Maria	763 451 4587 / 863 341 4123		

Physical Representation

ROW-1 : CF1 : Col1 : TS1 : David
ROW-1 : CF1 : Col2 : TS1 : 982 765 2345
ROW-3 : CF1 : Col1 : TS1 : Elan
ROW-4 : CF1 : Col1 : TS1 : Maria
ROW-4 : CF1 : Col2 : TS1 : 763 451 4587
ROW-4 : CF1 : Col2 : TS2 : 863 341 4123

Physical Representation

ROW-2 : CF2 : Col1 : TS1 : John
ROW-3 : CF2 : Col2 : TS1 : 909 451 4587
ROW-3 : CF2 : Col2 : TS2 : 823 441 4123

In HBase, the entire cell, along with the added structural information such as the row key and timestamp, is called the key value. Hence, each cell not only represents the column and data, but also the row key and timestamp stored.

While designing tables in HBase, we usually have two options to go for:

- Fewer rows with many columns (flat and wide tables)
- Fewer columns with many rows (tall and narrow tables)

Let's consider a use case where we need to store all the tweets made by a user in a single row. This approach might work for many users, but there will be users who will have a large magnitude of tweets in their account. In HBase, rows are identified by splitting them at boundaries. This also enforces the recommendation for tall and narrow tables that have fewer columns with many rows.

Hence, a better approach would be to store each tweet of a user in a separate row, where the row key should be the combination of the user ID and the tweet ID. Rows with fewer columns is just a logical representation, and physically, at the disk level, this makes no difference as all the values are stored in linear sets. Hence, even if the tweet ID is defined in the column qualifier or in the row key, each cell will ultimately contain a single tweet message.

Consider another use case of processing streaming events, which is a classic example of time series data. The source of streaming data could be any, for example, stock exchange real-time feeds, data coming from a sensor, or data coming from the network monitoring system for the production environment. While designing the table structure for the time series data, we usually consider the event's time as a row key.

In HBase, rows are stored in regions by sorting them in distinct ranges using specific start and stop keys. The sequentially increasing time series data gets written to the same region; this causes the issue of data being ingested onto a single region which is hosted on a region server, leading to a hotspot. This distribution of data instantly slows down the read/write performance of a cluster to the speed of a single server.

To solve this issue of data getting written to a single region server, an easy solution can be to prefix the row key with a nonsequential prefix and to ensure the distribution of data over all the region servers instead of just one. There are other approaches as well:

- **Salting**: The salting prefix can be used, along with a row key, to ensure that the data is stored across all the region servers. For example, we can generate a random salt number by taking the hash code of the timestamp and its modulus with any number of region servers. The drawback of this approach is that data reads are distributed across the region servers and need to be handled in a client code for the `get()` or `scan()` operation. An example of salting is shown in the following code:

```
int saltNumber = new Long(new Long(timestamp).hashCode()) %
<number of region servers>
byte[] rowkey = Bytes.add(Bytes.toBytes(saltNumber), Bytes.
toBytes(timestamp);
```

- **Hashing**: This approach is not suited for time series data, as by performing hashing on the timestamp, the certainty of losing the consecutive values arises and reading the data between the time ranges would not be possible.

HBase does not provide direct support for secondary indexes, but there are many use cases that require secondary indexes such as:

- A cell lookup using coordinates other than the row key, column family name, and qualifier
- Scanning a range of rows from the table ordered by the secondary index

Due to the lack of direct support, we can use the following approaches in HBase to create secondary indexes, which stores a mapping between the new coordinates and the existing coordinates:

- **Application-managed approach**: This approach suggests that you move the responsibility completely into the application or client layer. This approach deals with a data table and one or more lookup/mapping tables. Whenever the code writes into the data table, it also updates the lookup tables. The main advantage of this approach is that it provides full control over mapping the keys as the full logic of mapping is written at the client's end. However, this liberty also carries a cost: getting some orphaned mappings if any client process fails; cleaning orphaned mappings (using MapReduce) is another overhead as lookup/mapping tables also takes cluster space and consumes processing power.

- **Indexing solutions for HBase**: Other indexing solutions are also present to provide secondary index support in HBase, such as Lily HBase indexer, `http://ngdata.github.io/hbase-indexer/`. This solution quickly indexes HBase rows into Solr and provides the ability to easily search for any content stored in HBase. Such solutions do not require separate tables for each index, rather they maintain them purely in the memory. These solutions index the on-disk data, and during searches, only in-memory index related details are used for data. The main advantage of this solution is that the index is never out of sync.

 HBase provides an advanced feature called coprocessor that can also be used to achieve a behavior similar to that of secondary indexes. The coprocessor provides a framework for a flexible and generic extension for distributed computation directly within the HBase server processes.

HBase table scans

In the previous chapter, we took a look at CRUD operations in HBase. Now, let's take a step further and discuss table scans in Hbase. In Hbase, table scans are similar to iterators in Java or nonscrollable cursors in the RDBMS world. The HBase table scans command is useful for querying the data to access the complete set of records for a specific value by applying filters. Hence, the `scan()` operation reads the defined portion of data similar to the `get()` operation, and the filters are applied to the read portion for narrowing down the results further.

The `org.apache.hadoop.hbase.client` package provides the `Scan` class with the following constructors:

Constructor	Description
`Scan()`	The default scan constructor reads the entire HBase table, including all the column families and the respective columns
`Scan(byte[] startRow)`	Creates a scan operation starting at the specified row
`Scan(byte[] startRow, byte[] stopRow)`	Creates a scan operation for the range of rows specified, including the start row and excluding the stop row
`Scan(byte[] startRow, Filter filter)`	Creates a scan operation starting at the specified row and also applies the filter
`Scan(Get get)`	Builds a scan object with the same specifications as `Get`
`Scan(Scan scan)`	Creates a new instance of this class while copying all values

The behavior of the `scan()` operation looks similar to the `get()` operation, but the difference between the two is also very much visible through constructors. In the `get()` operation, we only define the row key to get the results, whereas in a scan, we can define the optional `startRow` parameter, which signifies the starting row key from where the scan needs to start reading data from the HBase table; this also makes the results inclusive of the start row. Similarly, the constructors also define the optional `stopRow` parameter, which limits the scan to a specific row key where it should conclude the reading, and the results exclude the stop row.

Hence, using the partial key scan by using the start and stop keys, it is possible to iterate over subsets of rows. We can also take an offset, limit the parameters, and apply them to the rows on the client side.

The `scan()` operation does not look for an exact match for the values defined for `startRow` and `stopRow`. The `scan()` operation matches the first row key for equality or greater than the given `startRow` value. In case no start row is specified, reading starts from the beginning of the table. Similarly, the current row key should also be equal to or greater than the `stopRow` value and in case no stop row is specified, the scan will read the data until the end of the table.

The scan() operation also defines one more optional parameter called filter. This filter is the instance of the Filter class present in the org.apache.hadoop.hbase. filter package.

 Filters limit data retrieval by adding limiting selectors to the get() or scan() operation. Filters will be discussed in detail in the following section.

Once we have the results from the scan constructor, the following methods can be used to further narrow down the results:

Method name	Description
addFamily(byte[] family)	Gets all columns from the specified family.
addColumn(byte[] family, byte[] qualifier)	Gets the column from the specific family with the specified qualifier.
setTimeRange(long minStamp, long maxStamp)	Gets versions of columns only within the specified timestamp range (minStamp, maxStamp).
setTimeStamp(long timestamp)	Gets versions of columns with the specified timestamp.
setMaxVersions(int maxVersions)	Gets up to the specified number of versions of each column. The default value of the maximum version returned is 1 which is the latest cell value.
setFilter(Filter filter)	Applies the specified server-side filter when performing the query.
setStartRow(byte[] startRow)	Sets the start row of the scan.
setStopRow(byte[] stopRow)	Sets the stop row.

As discussed, we have multiple constructors for the Scan class, but we do not have any method call for scanning the results within the HTable class. We need to call the getScanner() method available in the HTable class to get the instance of the scan and browse through the results.

Method	Description
getScanner(byte[] family)	Gets a scanner on the current table for the given family
getScanner(byte[] family, byte[] qualifier)	Gets a scanner on the current table for the given family and qualifier
getScanner(Scan scan)	Returns a scanner on the current table as specified by the Scan object

All the preceding methods return an instance of the `ResultScanner` class. This class provides a behavior similar to an iterator to the `Scan` class instance. The `Scan` instance does not obtain the complete results in a single call, as this could be a very heavy call to make. The following methods of the `ResultScanner` class help to achieve iterative behavior:

Method	Description
`close()`	Closes the scanner and releases any resources it has allocated
`next()`	Grabs the next row's worth of values
`next(int nbRows)`	Grabs the zero and nbRows results

The `next()` method returns the `Results` class to represent the row's contents. By default, the result is contained only for a single row and a fresh RPC call is made for each next call. To avoid too many calls, the `ResultScanner` class also provides the provision for row caching. Within the `hbase-site.xml` configuration file, we can set the following code:

```
<property>
<name>hbase.client.scanner.caching</name>
<value>5</value>
</property>
```

This property sets the row caching to 5 from the default value of 1 for all the scan calls. We can also set the caching limit for individual scan calls using the `setScannerCaching(int scannerCaching)` method on an `HTable` instance. This caching works at the row level and might not be a good option for the rows containing hundreds of columns. For limiting the columns returned on each `next()` call, we can use the following code:

```
void setBatch(int batch)
```

Using scanner caching and batch together provides control over the number of RPC calls required to scan the row key range selected.

Let's take a look at a complete example of the `Scan` usage:

```
public class ScanExample {
    public static void main(String[] args) throws IOException {
        // Get instance of Default Configuration
        Configuration conf = HBaseConfiguration.create();

        // Get table instance
        HTable table = new HTable(conf, "tab1");
```

```
    // Create Scan instance
    Scan scan = new Scan();

    // Add a column with value "Hello", in "cf1:greet",
    // to the Scan.
    scan.addColumn(Bytes.toBytes("cf1"), Bytes.toBytes("greet"));

    // Set Start Row
    scan.setStartRow(Bytes.toBytes("row-5"));

    // Set End Row
    scan.setStopRow(Bytes.toBytes("row-10"));

    // Get Scanner Results
    ResultScanner scanner = table.getScanner(scan);

    for (Result res : scanner) {
      System.out.println("Row Value: " + res);
    }
    scanner.close();
    table.close();
  }
}
```

This example returns row 5 to row 9 from the column family CF1 and the greet column.

Implementing filters

We apply column families, column qualifiers, timestamps, or ranges with the get() and scan() operations for limiting the data retrieved. Designing a row key to match the access patterns in every case is not possible, as at times we only need a subset of the data retrieved. Filters provide such a level of fine-grained access, that is, filtering the dataset based on some regular expression. The HBase API provides a filter interface and an abstract class, FilterBase, under the org.apache.hadoop.hbase. filter package, which is further extended by many classes such as CompareFilter, PageFilter, SkipFilter, TimeStampsFilter, and so on, to provide additional functionalities. The following method defined in the Scan class is used to set an instance of the filter:

- setFilter(Filter filter): Apply the specified server-side filter when performing the query

Typically, filters can be categorized into multiple types, as follows:

- Utility filters
- Comparison filters
- Custom filters

Utility filters

These types of filter classes provide the specific needs and directly extend the `FilterBase` class. Some of the utility filters are discussed as follows:

- `TimeStampFilter`: This filter returns the scan results with the cells whose timestamp (Version) is in the specified list of timestamps (Versions), as shown in the following code:

```
public class TSFilterExample {
public static void main(String[] args) throws IOException
{
    // Get instance of Default Configuration
    Configuration conf = HBaseConfiguration.create();

    // Get table instance
    HTable table = new HTable(conf, "tab1");

    // Add the timestamp range as minStamp and
    // maxStams.
    List<Long> ts = new ArrayList<Long>();
    ts.add(new Long(2));
    ts.add(new Long(10));

    // filter output the column values for
    // specified timestamps
    Filter filter = new TimestampsFilter(ts);

    // Create Scan instance
    Scan scan = new Scan();
    scan.setFilter(filter);

    // Get Scanner Results
    ResultScanner scanner = table.getScanner(scan);

    for (Result res : scanner) {
      System.out.println("Row Value: " + res);
    }
```

```
        scanner.close();
        table.close();
    }
}
```

- SingleColumnValueFilter and SingleColumnValueExcludedFilter: These filters keep track of a single column value, which if it exists, makes the row eligible to either be included or excluded from the results. It takes a CompareFilter.CompareOp operator (equal, greater, not equal, and so on) and either a byte[] value or ByteArrayComparable. Also, it takes a family and a qualifier, as shown in the following code:

```
public class SCVFilterExample {
public static void main(String[] args) throws IOException
{
    // Get instance of Default Configuration
Configuration conf = HBaseConfiguration.create();

    // Get table instance
    HTable table = new HTable(conf, "tab1");

    SingleColumnValueFilter filter = new
    SingleColumnValueFilter(
    Bytes.toBytes("cf1"), Bytes.toBytes("greet"),
    CompareFilter.CompareOp.EQUAL, new
    SubstringComparator("Hello"));

    // By Default it is false.
    // If set as true, this restricts the rows
    // if the specified column is not present
    filter.setFilterIfMissing(true);

    // Create Scan instance
    Scan scan = new Scan();
    scan.setFilter(filter);

    // Get Scanner Results
    ResultScanner scanner = table.getScanner(scan);

    for (Result res : scanner) {
      System.out.println("Row Value: " + res);
    }
    scanner.close();
    table.close();
    }
}
```

Some other useful utility filters are as follows:

- `PageFilter`: This filter keeps track of the number of rows returned per page. It terminates scanning once the number of filter-passed rows is greater than the given page size. This is because the filter is applied separately on different region servers.

- `ColumnCountGetFilter`: This filter restricts the number of columns returned for each row. This is more suitable for the `get()` operation, as in the case of the `scan()` operation, it stops as soon as it finds the row with the specified number of columns.

- `ColumnPaginationFilter`: This filter provides the pagination over the column within the rows. Using the offset parameter, it skips the specified number of columns.

- `RandomRowFilter`: This filter uses Java's `Random.nextFloat()` method for selecting the rows randomly.

Comparison filters

These types of filter use the comparison operator and comparator instance. The comparison operators, such as LESS, EQUAL, GREATER, and so on, define the inclusion or exclusion criteria for the applied filter. This provides fine-grained control to specify the range, subset, or exact match for the data scanned. Comparator instances, such as `BinaryComparator`, `RegexStringComparator`, `SubstringComparator`, and so on, are required to compare the cell values or keys. Some of the comparison filters are discussed as follows:

- `RowFilter`: This filter works based on the key value. It takes a comparison operator and a `byte[]` comparator for the row, as well as the column qualifier portions of a key, as shown in the following code:

```
public class RowFilterExample {
public static void main(String[] args) throws IOException
{
    // Get instance of Default Configuration
    Configuration conf = HBaseConfiguration.create();

    // Get table instance
    HTable table = new HTable(conf, "tab1");

    // Create Scan instance
    Scan scan = new Scan();
```

```
        // Add a column with value "Hello", in
        // "cf1:greet", to the scan.
        scan.addColumn(Bytes.toBytes("cf1"),
        Bytes.toBytes("greet"));

        // Filter using the regular expression
        Filter filter = new
        RowFilter(CompareFilter.CompareOp.EQUAL,
            new RegexStringComparator("*-o"));

        scan.setFilter(filter);


        // Get Scanner Results
        ResultScanner scanner = table.getScanner(scan);

        for (Result res : scanner) {
          System.out.println("Row Value: " + res);
        }
        scanner.close();
        table.close();
    }
}
```

- **ValueFilter**: This filter works based on a specific column value and only includes the rows where the column value passes the criteria. The following is the syntax:

```
// Filter using the sub-string expression
Filter filter = new ValueFilter(CompareFilter.CompareOp.NOT_EQUAL,
    New SubstringtringComparator("BYE"));
```

- **FamilyFilter**: This filter is very similar to RowFilter and is applied on column families in place of row keys. The following is the syntax:

```
// Filter in include the specific column families
Filter filter = new FamilyFilter(CompareFilter.CompareOp.GREATER,
    new BinaryComparator(Bytes.toBytes("cf1")));
```

Some other useful comparison filters are stated as follows:

- `DependentColumnFilter`: This filter adds the intercolumn timestamp, matching pattern and cells with a correspondingly timestamped entry in the target column, which will be part of the results. This filter only works with the `get()` operations and is not compatible with the batch feature of the `scan()` operations as this filter needs to cover all the columns of any row.

- `QualifierFilter`: This filter works based on a specific column qualifier and only includes the rows where the column qualifier passes the criteria.

Custom filters

These types of filters can be further categorized into two as follows:

- **Wrapper filters**: These filters typically extend or change the behavior of an existing filter to achieve more fine-grained control over the results. The HBase API provides the following wrapper filters:

  ○ `SkipFilter`: This filters an entire row if any of the cell checks do not pass. For example, filter out the entire row if any of its column values is zero. For example, refer to the following code:

    ```
    scan.setFilter(new SkipFilter(new ValueFilter (   CompareOp.
    NOT_EQUAL, new BinaryComparator( Bytes.toBytes(0))));
    ```

  ○ `WhileMatchFilter`: This filter returns `true` from `filterAllRemaining()` as soon as the wrapped filter, such as `RowFilter` or `ValueFilter`, matches true to the specified value and also stops the `scan()` operation.

- **Pure custom filters**: The HBase API covers most of the filter cases, but there might be the need to use a case-specific filtration of records. To address this, the API also provides the provision to write pure custom filters. These new filters can be written either by implementing the filter interface or by extending the `FilterBase` abstract class, which also implements the filter interface and provides the default implementation. Each method provided in the filter interface is used to retrieve rows during the `scan()` operation.

The following implementation shows the custom filter created for comparing the cell value with a specified value:

```
public class CustomFilterImpl extends FilterBase {

  private byte[] value = null;
  private boolean filterRow = true;

  public CustomFilterImpl() {
    super();
  }

  // Set the value to compare
  public CustomFilterImpl(byte[] value) {
    this.value = value;
  }

  // Reset filter flag for each row
  @Override
  public void reset() {
    this.filterRow = true;
  }

  @SuppressWarnings("deprecation")
  @Override
  public ReturnCode filterKeyValue(Cell cell) {
    // When there is a matching value, then let the row pass.
    if (Bytes.compareTo(value, cell.getValue()) == 0) {
      filterRow = false;
    }
    // Always use include.
    return ReturnCode.INCLUDE;
  }

  // Method for decision making based on the flag.
  @Override
  public boolean filterRow()
{
    return filterRow;
  }
```

```
      // Writes the given value out so it can be sent to the
      // region servers.
      public void write(DataOutput dataOutput) throws IOException {
      Bytes.writeByteArray(dataOutput, this.value);
   }

   // Used by region servers to establish the filter
   // instance with the correct values.
   public void readFields(DataInput dataInput) throws IOException
   {
      this.value = Bytes.readByteArray(dataInput);
   }
}
```

Summary

In this chapter, we learned about the advanced data modeling concepts such as understanding keys in HBase. We learned the basics of table scanning in HBase and the types of available filters. We also covered the application of these filters for table scan operations using examples.

In the next chapter, we will take a look at HBase storage and the replication architecture and also cover HBase over MapReduce in detail.

4
The HBase Architecture

In the previous chapters, we learned the basic building blocks of HBase schema designing and applying the CRUD operations over the designed schema. In this chapter, we will look at HBase from its architectural view point on the following topics:

- Data storage
- Data replication
- Securing HBase

For most of the developers or users, the preceding topics are not of big interest, but for an administrator, it really makes sense to understand how underlying data is stored or replicated within HBase. Administrators are the people who deal with HBase, starting from its installation to cluster management (performance tuning, monitoring, failure, recovery, data security, and so on).

By the end of this chapter, we will also get an insight into the integration of HBase and Map Reduce. Let's start with data storage in HBase first.

Data storage

In HBase, tables are split into smaller chunks that are distributed across multiple servers. These smaller chunks are called regions and the servers that host regions are called **RegionServers**. The master process handles the distribution of regions among RegionServers, and each RegionServer typically hosts multiple regions. In HBase implementation, the HRegionServer and HRegion classes represent the region server and the region, respectively. HRegionServer contains the set of HRegion instances available to the client and handles two types of files for data storage:

- HLog (the write-ahead log file, also known as WAL)
- HFile (the real data storage file)

In HBase, there is a system-defined catalog table called `hbase:meta` that keeps the list of all the regions for user-defined tables.

In older versions prior to 0.96.0, HBase had two catalog tables called `-ROOT-` and `.META`. The `-ROOT-` table was used to keep track of the location of the `.META` table. Version 0.96.0 onwards, the `-ROOT-` table is removed. The `.META` table is renamed as `hbase:meta`. Now, the location of `.META` is stored in ZooKeeper. The following is the structure of the `hbase:meta` table.

Key – the region key of the format (`[table]`, `[region start key]`, `[region id]`). A region with an empty start key is the first region in a table.

The values are as follows:

- `info:regioninfo` (serialized the `HRegionInfo` instance for this region)
- `info:server` (server:port of the RegionServer containing this region)
- `info:serverstartcode` (start time of the RegionServer process that contains this region)

When the table is split, two new columns will be created as `info:splitA` and `info:splitB`. These columns represent the two newly created regions. The values for these columns are also serialized as `HRegionInfo` instances. Once the split process is complete, the row that contains the old region information is deleted.

In the case of data reading, the client application first connects to ZooKeeper and looks up the location of the `hbase:meta` table. For the next client, the `HTable` instance queries the `hbase:meta` table and finds out the region that contains the rows of interest and also locates the region server that is serving the identified region. The information about the region and region server is then cached by the client application for future interactions and avoids the lookup process. If the region is reassigned by the load balancer process or if the region server has expired, a fresh lookup is done on the `hbase:meta` catalog table to get the new location of the user table region and the cache is updated accordingly.

At the object level, the `HRegionServer` class is responsible for creating a connection with the region by creating `HRegion` objects. This `HRegion` instance sets up a store instance that has one or more `StoreFile` instances (wrapped around HFile) and MemStore. MemStore accumulates the data edits as it happens and buffers them into the memory. This is also important for accessing the recent edits of the table data.

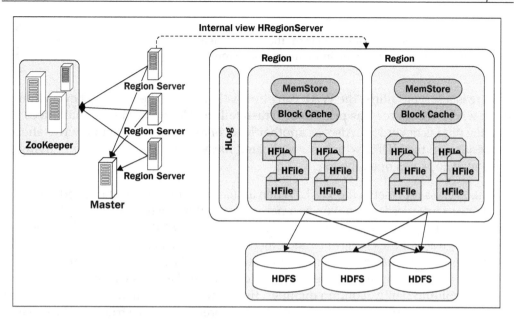

As shown in the preceding diagram, the HRegionServer instance (the region server) contains the map of HRegion instances (regions) and also has an HLog instance that represents the WAL. There is a single block cache instance at the region-server level, which holds data from all the regions hosted on that region server.

A block cache instance is created at the time of the region server startup and it can have an implementation of LruBlockCache, SlabCache, or BucketCache. The block cache also supports multilevel caching; that is, a block cache might have first-level cache, L1, as LruBlockCache and second-level cache, L2, as SlabCache or BucketCache. All these cache implementations have their own way of managing the memory; for example, LruBlockCache is like a data structure and resides on the JVM heap whereas the other two types of implementation also use memory outside of the JVM heap.

HLog (the write-ahead log – WAL)

In the case of writing the data, when the client calls HTable.put(Put), the data is first written to the write-ahead log file (which contains actual data and sequence numbers together represented by the HLogKey class) and also written in MemStore. Writing data directly into MemStrore can be dangerous as it is a volatile in-memory buffer and always open to the risk of losing data in case of a server failure. Once MemStore is full, the contents of the MemStore are flushed to the disk by creating a new HFile on the HDFS.

While inserting data from the HBase shell, the `flush` command can be used to write the in-memory (memstore) data to the store files.

If there is a server failure, the WAL can effectively retrieve the log to get everything up to where the server was prior to the crash failure. Hence, the WAL guarantees that the data is never lost. Also, as another level of assurance, the actual write-ahead log resides on the HDFS, which is a replicated filesystem. Any other server having a replicated copy can open the log.

The `HLog` class represents the WAL. When an `HRegion` object is instantiated, the single `HLog` instance is passed on as a parameter to the constructor of `HRegion`. In the case of an update operation, it saves the data directly to the shared WAL and also keeps track of the changes by incrementing the sequence numbers for each edit. WAL uses a Hadoop SequenceFile, which stores records as sets of key-value pairs. Here, the `HLogKey` instance represents the key, and the key-value represents the rowkey, column family, column qualifier, timestamp, type, and value along with the region and table name where data needs to be stored. Also, the structure starts with two fixed-length numbers that indicate the size and value of the key. The following diagram shows the structure of a key-value pair:

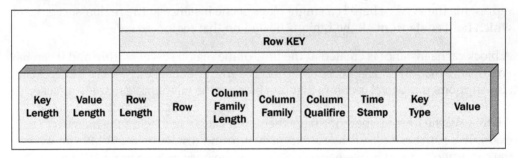

The `WALEdit` class instance takes care of atomicity at the log level by wrapping each update. For example, in the case of a multicolumn update for a row, each column is represented as a separate KeyValue instance. If the server fails after updating a few columns to the WAL, it ends up with only a half-persisted row and the remaining updates are not persisted. Atomicity is guaranteed by wrapping all updates that comprise multiple columns into a single `WALEdit` instance and writing it in a single operation.

For durability, a log writer's `sync()` method is called, which gets the acknowledgement from the low-level filesystem on each update. This method also takes care of writing the WAL to the replication servers (from one datanode to another). The log flush time can be set to as low as you want, or even be kept in sync for every edit to ensure high durability but at the cost of performance.

To take care of the size of the write-ahead log file, the `LogRoller` instance runs as a background thread and takes care of rolling log files at certain intervals (the default is 60 minutes). Rolling of the log file can also be controlled based on the size and `hbase.regionserver.logroll.multiplier`. It rotates the log file when it becomes 90 percent of the block size, if set to `0.9`.

HFile (the real data storage file)

HFile represents the real data storage file. The files contain a variable number of data blocks and a fixed number of file info blocks and trailer blocks. The index blocks records the offsets of the data and meta blocks. Each data block contains a magic header and a number of serialized KeyValue instances.

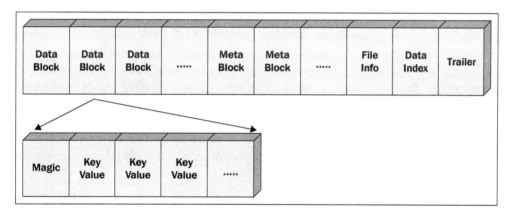

The default size of the block is 64 KB and can be as large as the block size. Hence, the default block size for files in HDFS is 64 MB, which is 1,024 times the HFile default block size but there is no correlation between these two blocks. Each key-value in the HFile is represented as a low-level byte array.

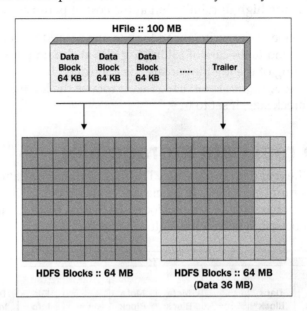

Within the HBase root directory, we have different files available at different levels. Write-ahead log files represented by the HLog instances are created in a directory called WALs under the root directory defined by the hbase.rootdir property in hbase-site.xml. This WALs directory also contains a subdirectory for each HRegionServer. In each subdirectory, there are several write-ahead log files (because of log rotation). All regions from that region server share the same HLog files.

In HBase, every table also has its own directory created under the data/default directory. This data/default directory is located under the root directory defined by the hbase.rootdir property in hbase-site.xml. Each table directory contains a file called .tableinfo within the .tabledesc folder. This .tableinfo file stores the metadata information about the table, such as table and column family schemas, and is represented as the serialized HTableDescriptor class. Each table directory also has a separate directory for every region comprising the table, and the name of this directory is created using the MD5 hash portion of a region name. The region directory also has a .regioninfo file that contains the serialized information of the HRegionInfo instance for the given region.

Once the region exceeds the maximum configured region size, it splits and a matching split directory is created within the region directory. This size is configured using the `hbase.hregion.max.filesize` property or the configuration is done at the column-family level using the `HColumnDescriptor` instance.

In the case of multiple flushes by the MemStore, the number of files might get increased on this disk. The compaction process running in the background combines the files to the largest configured file size and also triggers region split.

Data replication

Data replication is copying data from one cluster to another cluster by replicating the writes as the first cluster received it. Intercluster (geographically apart as well) replication in HBase is achieved by log shipping asynchronously. Data replication serves as a disaster recovery solution and also provides higher availability at the HBase layer.

The master-push pattern used by HBase replication keeps track of what is currently being replicated as each region server has its own write-ahead log. One master cluster can replicate any number of slave clusters. Each region server will participate to replicate its own batch (the default size is 64 MB) of write-ahead edit records contained within WAL.

The master-push pattern used for cluster replication can be designed in three different ways:

- **Master-slave replication**: In this type of replication, all the writes go to the primary cluster (master) first and then are replicated to the secondary cluster (slave). This type of enforcement is done at an application level as HBase does not ensure such replication. In case the application writes the data to a secondary cluster, data never gets replicated to the master cluster.

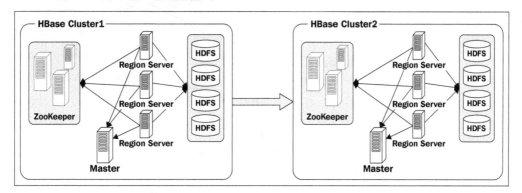

- **Master-master replication**: In this pattern, data can be written to any of the cluster as all the clusters are considered as a master as well as a slave. When a cluster receives the data, the remaining clusters get the replicated copy.

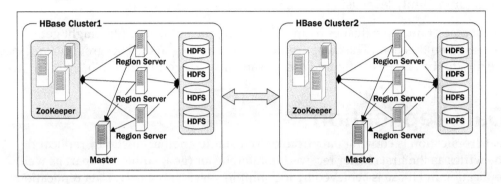

- **Cyclic replication**: This type of replication can be configured where multiple clusters are involved. Cyclic replication is considered for special cases where the third cluster has data coming from different sources into different tables and the end goal is to have an identical state across all the clusters. The replication between any two clusters can be either in the master-master or master-slave mode.

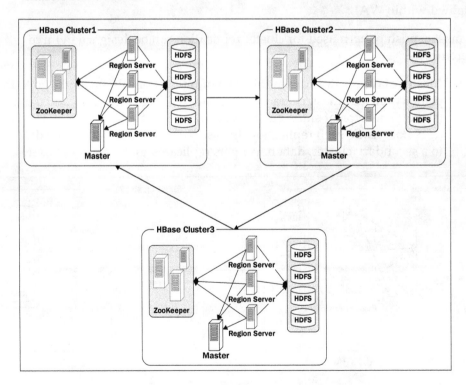

Every HBase cluster has a unique cluster ID stored on the file system to ensure that it does not change on restarts. This ID is used with master-master/acyclic replication. ZooKeeper plays an important role of coordinator in the HBase cluster replication process. Its coordination activity includes slave cluster registration, initiate replication, maintaining replication state, handling region server failovers, and so on.

When a master cluster region server initiates a replication source to a slave cluster, it first connects to the slave's ZooKeeper ensemble using the provided cluster ID. It then identifies region servers that are accepting incoming streams of edits to replicate by scanning the `/hbase/replication/rs` directory and randomly choose a subset of them.

If the slave region server does not respond to the RPC made by the master region server, the master region server will sleep and retry again until it reaches a configured number of retries. If the slave region server is still not available, the master cluster region server will select a new subset of the region server to replicate the data.

Replication configuration can be done at a column-family level by setting the replication scope to 1 at table-instantiation time or by altering the table. The same table name and column-family must exist on the secondary cluster. HBase won't create it if it doesn't exist, and the replication will fail. For more information on HBase replication, you can refer to `http://hbase.apache.org/book/cluster_replication.html`.

Securing HBase

With the default configuration, HBase does not provide any kind of data security. Even with the firewalls in place, HBase is not able to differentiate between multiple users coming from the same client, and uniform data access is provided to all the users. From HBase Version 0.92 onwards, HBase provides optional support for both user authentication and authorization. For user authentication, it provides integration points with Kerberos and for authorization, it provides access an controller coprocessor.

Kerberos is a networked authentication protocol designed to provide strong authentication for client/server applications by using secret-key cryptography. Kerberos uses **Kerberos Key Distribution Center** (**KDC**) as the authentication server and access ticket granting server. The setup of KDC is not in the scope of this book.

The access controller coprocessor is only implemented at the RPC level, and it is based on the **Simple Authentication and Security Layer** (**SASL**); the SASL that allows authentication, encryption negotiation, and/or message integrity verification on a per connection basis. To enable security in HBase, first set `hbase.security.authentication` as `true`. This property will enable the authentication only for HBase. As HBase uses Hadoop Distributed File System as the storage layer, `hadoop.security.authentication` should also be set as `true`.

Enabling authentication

To enable authentication, perform the following steps:

1. Add the following property to `hbase-site.xml` on every HBase server host (Master or RegionServer) and HBase client host as follows:

```
<property>
    <name>hbase.security.authentication</name>
    <value>kerberos</value>
</property>
<property>
  <name>hbase.security.authorization</name>
  <value>true</value>
</property>

<property>
<name>hbase.rpc.engine</name        <value>org.apache.hadoop.hbase.
ipc.SecureRpcEngine
</value>
</property>
```

2. For authentication, a `keytab` file is required that contains a key used to get authenticated to KDC. Use the syntax as `<username>/<fully.qualified.domain.name>@<YOUR-REALM>`. It is preferred to use `hbase` as the user name.

3. Create the HBase Kerberos service principal as:

```
kadmin: addprinc -randkey hbase/fully.qualified.domain.name@YOUR-REALM.COM
```

4. Create a `keytab` file as:

```
kadmin: xst -k hbase.keytab hbase/fully.qualified.domain.name
```

5. Copy the keytab file to the conf directory of all the HBase server host and make the hbase user as the owner of the keytab file with the read only permissions. Add the following entries to the hbase-site.xml configuration file on all of the cluster hosts running the HBase:

```
<property>                 <name>hbase.regionserver.kerberos.principal
   </name>
  <value>hbase/_HOST@YOUR-REALM.COM</value>
</property>

<property>
  <name>hbase.regionserver.keytab.file</name>
  <value>/etc/hbase/conf/hbase.keytab</value>
</property>

<property>
  <name>hbase.master.kerberos.principal</name>
  <value>hbase/_HOST@YOUR-REALM.COM</value>
</property>

<property>
<name>hbase.master.keytab.file</name>
<value>/etc/hbase/conf/hbase.keytab</value>
</property>
```

Enabling authorization

Perform the following steps to enable authorization:

1. Add the following property to hbase-site.xml on every HBase server host (Master or RegionServer) as follows:

```
<property>
      <name>hbase.security.authorization</name>
      <value>true</value>
</property>
<property>
<name>hbase.coprocessor.master.classes</name>     <value>org.
apache.hadoop.hbase.security.access.AccessController</value>
</property>
<property>
<name>hbase.coprocessor.region.classes</name>     <value>org.
apache.hadoop.hbase.security.token.TokenProvider,org.apache.
hadoop.hbase.security.access.AccessController
</value>
</property>
```

2. Set up the access control list as follows:

```
grant <user> <permissions>[ <table>[ <column family>[ <column
qualifier> ] ] ]    #grants permissions

revoke <user> <permissions> [ <table> [ <column family> [ <column
qualifier> ] ] ]   # revokes permissions

alter <table> {OWNER => <user>} # sets the table owner

user_permission <table>  # displays existing permissions
```

Here, permissions can be defined as follows:

- R (read permissions): This is required for the Get, Scan, or Exists calls
- W (write permissions): This is required for the Put, Delete, LockRow, UnlockRow, IncrementColumnValue, CheckAndDelete, and CheckAndPut calls
- C (create permissions): This is required for the Create, Alter, Drop, and Bulk Load calls
- A (admin permissions): This is required for the Enable, Disable, Flush, Split, Snapshot/Restore/Clone, MajorCompact, Grant, Revoke, and Shutdown calls
- E (execute permission): To execute coprocessor endpoints

The following is an example where permissions are defined:

```
hbase> grant 'user1', 'RW', 'EmployeeTable'
```

Once authentication and authorization is enabled, restart the HBase cluster. For encrypted communication, the following configuration can also be added to hbase-site.xml:

```
<property>
   <name>hbase.rpc.protection</name>
   <value>privacy</value>
</property>
```

We can use the Java code as follows;

```
Configuration conf = HBaseConfiguration.create();
conf.set("hbase.rpc.protection", "privacy");
HTable table = new HTable(conf, tablename);
```

Different configurations are required for the different types of clients. The following section only discusses the configuration required for REST-based clients.

Configuring REST clients

The following are the steps for the configuration of the REST-based clients:

1. Add the following to the `hbase-site.xml` file for every REST gateway server:

```
<property>
  <name>hbase.rest.keytab.file</name>
  <value><KEYTAB></value>
</property>
<property>
  <name>hbase.rest.kerberos.principal</name>
  <value><user>/HOST@HADOOP.LOCALDOMAIN</value>
</property>
```

2. Place the value for `<KEYTAB>` and `<user>`. Also, provide the REST API principal, `rest_server`, the administrative level of access as follows:

```
hbase> grant 'rest_server', 'RWCA'
```

3. Also, add the following configurations to the `base-site.xml` file for every HBase server as follows:

```
<property>
  <name>hadoop.security.authorization</name>
  <value>true</value>
</property>
<property>
  <name>hadoop.proxyuser.<USER>.groups</name>
  <value><GROUPS></value>
</property>
<property>
  <name>hadoop.proxyuser.<USER>.hosts</name>
  <value><GROUPS></value>
</property>
```

4. Place the values for `<users>` and `<groups>` and add the following configurations to the `base-site.xml` file for every REST gateway server as follows:

```
<property>
  <name>hbase.rest.authentication.type</name>
  <value>kerberos</value>
</property>
<property>
```

```
    <name>hbase.rest.authentication.kerberos.principal</name>
    <value>HTTP/HOST@HADOOP.LOCALDOMAIN</value>
  </property>
  <property>
    <name>hbase.rest.authentication.kerberos.keytab</name>
    <value><KEYTAB></value>
  </property>
```

5. Place the value for `<KEYTAB>`. Once all the configurations are done, restart the REST gateway and start playing with secure HBase from the REST-based client based on the access provided.

HBase and MapReduce

HBase has a close integration with Hadoop's MapReduce as it is built on top of the Apache Hadoop framework. Hadoop's MapReduce provides a distributed computation for high throughput data access, and **Hadoop Distributed File System (HDFS)** provides HBase with the storage layer with high availability, reliability, and durability for data.

Before we go into more details of how HBase integrates with Hadoop's MapReduce framework, let's first understand how this framework actually works.

Hadoop MapReduce

There should be a system to process terabytes or petabytes of data and increase its performance linearly with the number of physical machines added. Apache Hadoop's MapReduce framework is designed to provide linearly scalable processing power for huge amounts of Big Data.

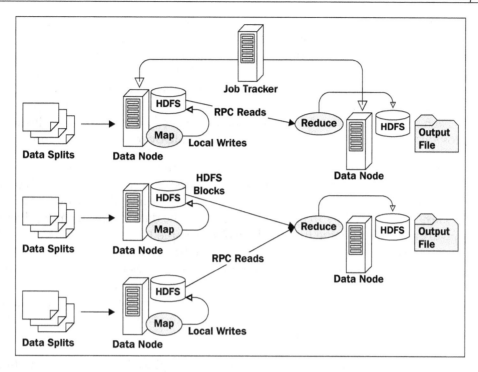

Let's discuss how MapReduce processes the data described in the preceding diagram. In MapReduce, the first step is the split process, which is responsible for dividing the input data into reasonably sized chunks that are then processed as a single map task. The JobTracker process acts as a manager application and is responsible for managing the MapReduce applications that run on the cluster. Jobs are submitted to JobTracker for execution, and it manages them by distributing the workload. It also keeps a track of all elements of the job, ensuring that failed tasks are either retried or resubmitted. Multiple MapReduce applications can also be run on a single Hadoop cluster, and the additional responsibility of JobTracker is to oversee resource utilization as well.

The `InputFormat` class is responsible for splitting the input data by calling `createRecordReader()` as many times as it is split and returning the `RecordReader` instance that defines the classes of the key and value objects. In the case of HBase, the specialized class, `TableInputFormat`, is provided that extends the abstract class, `TableInputFormatBase`. It iterates over the splits and creates a new `TableRecordReader` interface by calling `createRecordReader()` for each split. Hence, each `TableRecordReader` instance handles exactly one region. This instance also provides the `next()` method that is used to iterate over each input record.

All computations are implemented as either maps or reduce tasks. Here, each task operates over a portion of the total input data and does not communicate with other tasks. The `Mapper` class reads a specific type of the key-value pair. The output of a `Mapper` class is processed by the `reducer` class after the data has been shuffled and sorted. During the shuffle, the intermediate data is copied from the servers that run the map task to the servers that run the reduce tasks. Next, the sort operation combines the shuffled data so that the `reducer` class receives the intermediate data as a sorted set. In this sorted set, each unique key is associated with all of the possible values found during the processing. Here, the `OutputFormat` class' job is to persist the data at various data nodes. In the case of HBase, the `TableOutputFormat` class is used to allow output to HBase tables.

Hadoop is also optimized for minimal network I/O, that is, it brings the computation as close as possible to the data. In a typical Hadoop cluster, HDFS DataNodes and MapReduce `TaskTrackers` are placed on the same box that allows the map and reduce tasks to run on the same physical node where the data is located. By using this approach, Hadoop avoids transferring the data over the network. If the same physical node is not available, preference is given to the same rack.

In HDFS, data once written are immutable; therefore, data is written into new files, and as the file count grows, it becomes difficult for HBase to access the data. Hence, HBase performs housekeeping at regular intervals and compacts them into another set of new, consolidated files.

Running MapReduce over HBase

Coming back to HBase and Hadoop MapReduce framework integration, preferably RegionServers are collocated with HDFS DataNodes on the same physical hardware for data locality so that the region server reads and writes to the local DataNode as the primary DataNode.

For testing purposes, an additional library (.jar files) required by the job that is not available with the Hadoop codebase should be installed locally on the task tracker machines. Copy the JAR files on all the nodes at a common location.

Add the JAR files with the full path into the hadoop-env.sh configuration file, into the HADOOP_CLASSPATH variable:

```
#export HADOOP_CLASSPATH = "<additional_jars>:$HADOOP_
CLASSPATH"
```

Restart all task trackers for the changes to be effective. This method is not at all recommended for production environments.

While implementing Mapper, Reducer, and main driver class, these guidelines should be followed:

- The Mapper class:
    - The Mapper class should extend the TableMapper class
    - The map method of the Mapper class takes the rowkey of the Hbase table as an input key
    - The define input key is the ImmutableBytesWritable object
    - Another parameter, the org.apache.hadoop.hbase.client.Result object contains the input values as column/column-families from the HBase table

- The Reducer class
    - The Mapper class should extend the TableReducer class
    - The output key is defined as NULL
    - The output value is defined as the org.apache.hadoop.hbase.client.Put object.

- The Main class
    - Configure the org.apache.hadoop.hbase.client.Scan object and optionally define parameters such as start row, stop row, row filter, columns, and the column-families for the scan object.
    - Set the record caching size (the default is 1, which is not preferred for MapReduce) for scan object.

- ○ Set the block cache for scan object as `false`.
- ○ Define the input table using the `TableMapReduceUtil.initTableMapperJob` method. This method takes the source table name, scan object, the `Mapper` class name, `MapOutputKey`, `MapOutputValue`, and the `Job` object.
- ○ Define the input table using `TableMapReduceUtil.initTableReducerJob`. This method takes the target table name, the `Reducer` class name and the `Job` object.

HBase integrates with the MapReduce framework in three different ways, where HBase can be used as a data source to feeding the job, as a data sink to store the job results, or as a dual role of both data source and sink.

 Learning the MapReduce programming is out of scope of this book, and the following three sections can only be useful for experienced MapReduce programmers.

HBase as a data source

HBase as a data source can use the `TableInputFormat` class that sets up a table as an input to the MapReduce process. Here, the `Mapper` class extends the `TableMapper` class that sets the output key and value types as follows:

```
static class HBaseTestMapper extends TableMapper<Text, IntWritable>
```

Then, in the job execution method, `main()`, create and configure a `Scan` instance and set up the table mapper phase using the supplied utility as:

```
Scan scan = new Scan();
scan.setCaching(250);
scan.setCacheBlocks(false);


Job job = new Job(conf, "Read data from " + table);
job.setJarByClass(HBaseMRTest.class);

TableMapReduceUtil.initTableMapperJob(table, scan,
HBaseSourceTestMapper.class, Text.class, IntWritable.class, job);
```

The code shows how to use the `TableMapReduceUtil` class with its static methods to quickly configure a job with all the required classes.

HBase as a data sink

HBase as a data sink can also use the `TableOutputFormat` class that sets up a table as an output to the MapReduce process as:

```
Job job = new Job(conf, "Writing data to the " + table);

job.setOutputFormatClass(TableOutputFormat.class);
job.getConfiguration().set(TableOutputFormat.OUTPUT_TABLE, table);
```

The preceding lines also uses an implicit write buffer set up by the `TableOutputFormat` class. The call to `context.write()` issues an internal `table.put()` interface with the given instance of `Put`. The `TableOutputFormat` class also takes care of calling `flushCommits()` when the job is complete.

In a typical MapReduce usage with HBase, a reducer is not usually needed as data is already sorted and has unique keys to be stored in the HBase tables. If a reducer is required for certain use cases, it should extend the `TableReducer` class that again sets the input key and value types as:

```
static class HBaseSourceTestReduce extends TableReducer<.,.>
```

Also, set it in the job configuration as:

```
TableMapReduceUtil.initTableReducerJob("customers", HBaseTestReduce.
class, job);
```

Here, the writes go to the region that is responsible for the rowkey that is being written by the reduce task.

HBase as a data source and sink

This use case is the mix of both, that is, HBase as a data source as well as a data sink. Let's look at the complete code example that uses HBase as a source as well as a sink. This example reads the records from the `Customer` table for column-families `cf1` and copies it to another table, `CustomerTableCopy`:

```
package com.ch4;

import java.io.IOException;
import java.util.HashMap;

import org.apache.hadoop.conf.Configuration;
import org.apache.hadoop.hbase.KeyValue;
import org.apache.hadoop.hbase.client.Put;
import org.apache.hadoop.hbase.client.Result;
```

```
import org.apache.hadoop.hbase.client.Scan;
import org.apache.hadoop.hbase.io.ImmutableBytesWritable;
import org.apache.hadoop.hbase.mapreduce.TableMapReduceUtil;
import org.apache.hadoop.hbase.mapreduce.TableMapper;
import org.apache.hadoop.hbase.mapreduce.TableReducer;
import org.apache.hadoop.hbase.util.Bytes;
import org.apache.hadoop.io.IntWritable;
import org.apache.hadoop.io.Text;
import org.apache.hadoop.mapreduce.Job;

public class HBaseMRTest {

  // Mapper Class
  static class HBaseTestMapper extends TableMapper<Text, IntWritable>
{

    private final IntWritable ONE = new IntWritable(1);
    private Text text = new Text();

    @SuppressWarnings("deprecation")
    @Override
    public void map(ImmutableBytesWritable rowKey, Result columns,
        Context context) throws IOException, InterruptedException {
      try {

        HashMap<String, String> customerMap = new HashMap<String,
String>();
        for (KeyValue kv : columns.raw()) {
          String qualifier = "";
          HashMap<?, ?> kvMap = (HashMap<?, ?>) kv.toStringMap();
          String colFamily = (String) kvMap.get("family");
          if (colFamily.equalsIgnoreCase("cf1")) {
            if (kvMap.get("qualifier") != null
                && !kvMap.get("qualifier").equals("")) {
              qualifier = (String) kvMap.get("qualifier");
            }
            String qualifierVal = Bytes
                .toString(kv.getValueArray());
            customerMap.put(qualifier, qualifierVal);
          }
        }
        System.out.println(customerMap.toString());
```

```
      text.set(rowKey.toString());
      context.write(text, ONE);

    } catch (RuntimeException e) {
      e.printStackTrace();
    }
  }
}


// Reducer Class
static class HBaseTestReducer extends
TableReducer<Text, IntWritable, ImmutableBytesWritable> {

  protected void reduce(Text rowKey, Iterable<IntWritable> columns,
      Context context) throws IOException, InterruptedException {
    try {
      for (IntWritable values : columns) {
        System.out.println(values);
      }
      Put put = new Put(Bytes.toBytes(rowKey.toString()));
      put.add(Bytes.toBytes("cf1"), Bytes.toBytes("col-1"),
          Bytes.toBytes(rowKey.toString()));

      context.write(null, put);

    } catch (Exception e) {
      e.printStackTrace();
    }
  }
}


// Main Driver Class
@SuppressWarnings("deprecation")
public static void main(String[] args) throws Exception {

  try {

    // Setup Configuraiton
    Configuration config = new Configuration();
    config.clear();
    config.set("hbase.zookeeper.quorum", "localhost");
    config.set("hbase.zookeeper.property.clientPort", "2181");
    config.set("hbase.master", "localhost:60000");
```

```
Job job = new Job(config, "Read Write from Customer Table");
job.setJarByClass(HBaseMRTest.class);

Scan scan = new Scan();
// 1 is the default in Scan
scan.setCaching(1000);
scan.setCacheBlocks(false);

// define input hbase table
TableMapReduceUtil.initTableMapperJob(
  "tab1", // input table
    scan, // Scan instance to control CF and attribute selection
    HBaseTestMapper.class, // mapper class
    Text.class, // mapper output key
    IntWritable.class, // mapper output value
    job);

// define output table
TableMapReduceUtil.initTableReducerJob(
    "tab1Copy", // output table
    HBaseTestReducer.class, // reducer class
    job);

System.exit(job.waitForCompletion(true) ? 0 : 1);

} catch (Exception e) {
System.out.println("MR Execution Error");
System.exit(1);
}
}
}
```

Build the JAR file and run the `hadoop jar` command for `HBaseMRTestclass`. This will populate the data to the output HBase table, `tab1copy`. MapReduce can be used with HBase for many use cases such as data import/export between the HBase table and files, data consolidation, and so on.

Summary

In this chapter, we have learned the internals of HBase about how it stores the data. We also learned the basics of HBase cluster replication. In the last part, we got an overview of Hadoop MapReduce and covered the MapReduce execution over HBase using examples.

In the next chapter, we will look into the HBase advanced API used for counters and coprocessors, along with advanced configurations.

5
The HBase Advanced API

It is time to understand the power the API HBase provides. In this chapter, we are going to cover the advance HBase API used for the client application, as well as for the administrative operations. The following are the topics that will be covered in this chapter:

- Counters
- Coprocessors
- The administrative API

Let's start with counters first.

Counters

In the Web 2.0 world, most of the e-commerce applications collect statistics such as user clicks, likes, views, and so on. Earlier this data used to be collected from the application logfiles, which were subsequently analyzed to get the results.

Counters are another advanced and useful feature provided by HBase. Counters allow us to increment a column value with the least overhead by providing a mechanism to treat columns as counters. Using counters enables the potential of real-time accounting and completely takes away the offline batch-oriented logfile analysis.

Normally, incrementing column values requires steps such as locking the row, reading, incrementing, writing the value, and finally releasing the row for other writers. These steps cause a lot of I/O overheads and wait for other writers. Counters avoid all these I/O-centric steps by synchronizing the write operation over a row and incrementing values under a single row lock. Therefore, counters work only with a single row.

> The older version of HBase supports only a single counter update per RPC call but in newer versions, the client API supports updating multiple counters per RPC call. In the case of multiple counters as well, the RPC call is limited to a single row only.

Let's see the counter's behavior at the column level. The following code is the format to increment the column value as a counter using HBase shells for the incr command:

```
incr '<table>', '<row>', '<column>', [<increment-value>]
```

The following commands show the creation of a table, 'mycounters', and then increments a column, monthly:hits, value twice and the last value in the last query:

```
hbase(main):001:0> create 'mycounters', 'monthly'
0 row(s) in 3.1950 seconds

hbase(main):002:0>incr 'mycounters', 'Jan14', monthly:hits', 50
COUNTER VALUE = 50

hbase(main):003:0>incr 'mycounters', 'Jan14', monthly:hits', 100
COUNTER VALUE = 150

hbase(main):04:0>get_counter 'mycounters', 'Jan14', monthly:hits'
COUNTER VALUE = 150
```

Each call to incr returns the incremented value of the monthly:hits counter and finally checks the current value of the monthly:hits counter using the get_counter command.

> Note that counters can be incremented by one or any other value.

The default value of the counters is zero; hence, counters are not initialized at the time of creation. In the previous chapter, it was discussed that the PUT command is used to change the value for any column in HBase, but as a matter of precaution, it is mandatory to use the incr command to increment the counter type column value. The PUT command stores the value in a different format, which gives an erroneous value while accessing. We can also use the GET command in place of get_counter to access the counter value as follows:

```
hbase(main):005:0>get 'mycounters', 'Jan14'
COLUMN               CELL
daily:hits timestamp=1408810501368,value=\x00\x00\x00\x00\x00\x00\x00\xAA
1 row(s) in 0.0140 seconds
```

The preceding output also proves that counters are treated as only columns. However, the GET command provides the byte array representation as hexadecimal values, whereas using `get_counter` shows the current value in a human-readable format. Finally, counters are not only meant for incremental values but also for decremental values as well or they can be omitted completely.

```
hbase(main):04:0>incr 'mycounters', 'Jan14', monthly:hits', -4
COUNTER VALUE = 146
```

The following Java code shows the handling of counters:

```
package com.ch5;

import java.io.IOException;
import org.apache.hadoop.conf.Configuration;
import org.apache.hadoop.hbase.HBaseConfiguration;
import org.apache.hadoop.hbase.client.HTable;
import org.apache.hadoop.hbase.util.Bytes;

public class HbaseCounterExample {
  /**
   * Example for incrementing counter value.
   */
  Public static void main(String[] args) throws IOException {
    Configuration conf = HBaseConfiguration.create();
    HTable table = new HTable(conf, "mycounters");
    table.incrementColumnValue(Bytes.toBytes("Jan14"), Bytes.
toBytes("monthly"),
        Bytes.toBytes("hits"), 10L);

    table.close();
  }
}
```

The preceding Java program shows how we can increment the counter value using the HBase API method, `incrementColumnValue()`.

HBase provides two types of counters, namely:

- Single counters
- Multiple counters

Single counters

Under this type, a single RPC call is made to increment the value for a single counter only. The following are the methods provided by HTable for single counter handling:

```
long incrementColumnValue(byte[] row, byte[] family, byte[] qualifier,
long amount)
```

```
long incrementColumnValue(byte[] row, byte[] family, byte[] qualifier,
long amount, Durability durability)
```

The preceding methods increment the column value as an atomic operation. For these atomic operations, durability can be set as ASYNC_WAL, FSYNC_WAL, SKIP_WAL, SYNC_WAL, or USE_DEFAULT. Each value guarantees different levels of durability for the table. For example, Durability.SKIP_WAL means that in a fail scenario, any increments that have not been flushed will be lost. The following code samples show the usage of the methods:

```
HTable table = new HTable(conf, "counters");


long cnt1 = table.incrementColumnValue(Bytes.toBytes("Jan14"),Bytes.
toBytes("monthly"), Bytes.toBytes("hits"), 100, Durability.SKIP_WAL);


long cnt2 = table.incrementColumnValue(Bytes.toBytes("Feb14"),Bytes.
toBytes("monthly"), Bytes.toBytes("hits"), 1500, Durability.SKIP_WAL);
```

Multiple counters

In the case of multiple counters, a single RPC call is made to increment the value of multiple counters. HTable defines a method, increment(), which is used to increment the value of multiple counters:

```
Result increment(Increment increment)
```

This method increments one or more column values within a single row. These increments are done within a single row lock by making the write operations to a row as synchronized. While reading the values from HBase columns, clients do not take row locks; therefore, the get and scan operations might return the partially completed values. This method requires instances of the Increment class with all the appropriate details as follows:

```
Increment(byte[] row)

Increment(byte[] row, int offset, int length)
```

The preceding methods create an `Increment` operation for the specified row. A row key is provided while instantiating an `Increment` object. This row key represents the row that contains all the counters to be modified by making a subsequent call to the `increment()` method. Once the `Increment` instance is created, addition of the counters or columns to be incremented are added using the following method:

```
Increment addColumn(byte[] family, byte[] qualifier, long amount)
```

The following are examples of multiple counters:

```
Increment increment = new Increment(Bytes.toBytes("Jan14"));

increment.addColumn(Bytes.toBytes("monthly"), Bytes.toBytes("hits"), 10);

increment.addColumn(Bytes.toBytes("monthly"), Bytes.toBytes("hits"), 1);

increment.addColumn(Bytes.toBytes("monthly"), Bytes.toBytes("hits"), 20);

Result result = table.increment(increment);
```

Coprocessors

In an HBase cluster, the most computationally expensive portion of reading or writing operations happens when we apply server-side filters on scan results; although, this computation is very much specific to accessing the data. Similarly, with the coprocessor, we can move a part of the computation to where the data lives, like in the case of Hadoop, which works in a distributed way for data storage (HDFS), as well as data processing (MapReduce). Using HBase coprocessors, custom features such as secondary indexing, complex filtering and access control features can be developed.

HBase coprocessor-based code run in parallel across all RegionServers and convert the cluster from horizontally scalable storage to a highly capable, distributed, data storage and data-processing system. The HBase coprocessor's design is inspired by Google's BigTable coprocessor's design.

In an HBase cluster, coprocessor works in two different scopes:

- System level: These coprocessors can be loaded globally on any or all tables and regions hosted by the region server
- Table level: These coprocessors can be loaded on all regions of a table on a per table basis

To provide flexibility, the coprocessor framework provides two different categories of coprocessor extensions as:

- The observer coprocessor
- The endpoint coprocessor

The observer coprocessor

Observer coprocessors are like triggers in the database world. They allow the cluster to behave differently during normal execution of client operations, for example, an observer coprocessor layered between the client and HBase to influence the data access at run time. Another example, is running an observer coprocessor after every Get command to modify the result returned to the client at run time or after a Put command and manipulating data before it's persisted. Multiple observers can be registered simultaneously and their priorities can be defined for execution. The CoprocessorHost class manages observer registration and execution on behalf of the region.

Based on the HBase architecture, observer coprocessors can further be categorized into the following types:

- RegionObserver: As the name suggests, RegionObserver runs on the region and a multiple RegionObserver coprocessor can be registered to run on the same RegionServer. RegionObserver provides a hook for data manipulation operations such as Get, Put, Delete, Scan, and so on. These data-manipulation commands can be executed along with both pre and post observers. It also defines the pre and post hooks for internal operations such as flushing MemStore and splitting the region. The configuration property, hbase. coprocessor.region.classes, can be set to register the region observer.

- RegionServerObserver: This observer provides the pre and post hooks for the merge, commits, and rollback operations and runs within the context of the HBase region server. This coprocessor can be registered using the hbase. coprocessor.regionserver.classes configuration property.

- WALObserver: This observer provides hooks for the write-ahead log (WAL) and support for the pre and post WAL write events. The WALObserver coprocessor always runs in the context of WAL processing on a region server and can be registered by setting the hbase.coprocessor.wal.classes configuration property.

- `MasterObserver`: This observer provides hooks for data definition type operations such as table creation, deletion, schema modification, and so on. The `MasterObserver` coprocessor runs within the context of HBase Master and can be registered by setting the `hbase.coprocessor.master.classes` configuration property.

For each type of observer coprocessor, a base abstract class is defined that implements the default behavior for the methods declared in the implemented interface. For example, `BaseRegionObserver` implements all the methods with the default behavior declared in the `RegionObserver` interface. Similarly, `BaseMasterObserver` implements all the methods with the default behavior declared in the `MasterObserver` interface. This provides the flexibility of overriding only in the focus methods without worrying about implementing the rest of the methods. The following skeleton code shows how to implement a coprocessor by extending the base abstract classes:

```
package com.ch5;

import java.io.IOException;
import java.util.List;
import org.apache.hadoop.hbase.KeyValue;
import org.apache.hadoop.hbase.client.Get;
import org.apache.hadoop.hbase.coprocessor.BaseRegionObserver;
import org.apache.hadoop.hbase.coprocessor.ObserverContext;
import org.apache.hadoop.hbase.coprocessor.
RegionCoprocessorEnvironment;
import org.apache.hadoop.hbase.security.AccessDeniedException;

// Sample access-control observer coprocessor. It utilizes       //
RegionObserverand intercept preGet() method to check user        //
privilege for the given table and column family.

Public class ObserverCoprocessorEx extends BaseRegionObserver {
// @Override
Public void preGet(ObserverContext<RegionCoprocessorEnvironment> c,Get
get, List<KeyValue> result) throws IOException {
byte[] region = c.getEnvironment().getRegion().getRegionInfo()
        .getRegionName();
// TODO Code for checking the permissions over
// table or region...
    if (ACCESS_NOT_ALLOWED) {
throw new AccessDeniedException("User is not allowed for access");
    }
  }
// Similarly override prePut(), preDelete(), etc. based on the
// need.
}
```

Finally, register the coprocessor as follows:

```
<property>
<name>ObserverCoprocessorEx</name>
<value>com.ch5.ObserverCoprocessorEx</value>
</property>
```

To register multiple coprocessors, a comma-separated list needs to be provided with the value property. Once the coprocessor is registered, the status of a coprocessor can also be checked using the following HBase shell command:

```
hbase(main):020:0>status 'ObserverCoprocessorEx'
```

The endpoint coprocessor

Endpoint coprocessors are powerful and store procedures, such as features provided by HBase. These coprocessors can be invoked at any time from the client. Once invoked, the endpoint coprocessor implementation will be executed at the target region or regions and will return the results to the calling client.

The endpoint coprocessor is also an interface to dynamically extend the RPC protocol used by HBase. Once the endpoint coprocessor implementation is installed, it unfolds additional methods to the client. Using these extensions, new features can be added to HBase without modifying or recompiling HBase binaries. These endpoints are defined and callable as "**protocol buffers (protobuf)**" services.

> Protocol buffers are Google's language-neutral, platform-neutral, extensible mechanism to serialize structured data. Once the structure for the data is defined, it can be easily written and read, using special generated source code to and from a variety of data streams and using a variety of languages — Java, C++, or Python. For more details, refer to https://developers.google.com/protocol-buffers/.

The following steps need to be performed to build a custom endpoint coprocessor:

1. Define the coprocessor service and the supporting message types for the RPC methods in a `.proto` file.

2. Run the `protoc` command to generate the service and message code.

3. Provide implementation for the following:

    o   Implement the protobuf service interface

    o   Create a new `org.apache.hadoop.hbase.coprocessor.CoprocessorService` interface. This interface is required to register the exposed service with `RegionCoprocessorHost`.

4. Finally, the client calls the `CoprocessorService.getService()` method that should return a reference to the endpoint's protocol buffer service instance.

 Refer to the API documentation on the coprocessor package at `http://hbase.apache.org/devapidocs/org/apache/hadoop/hbase/coprocessor/package-frame.html`, and for an example, refer to the details in `/hbase-examples/src/test/java/org/apache/hadoop/hbase/coprocessor/example/` of the HBase source code.

The administrative API

So far, we have only talked about the API used by the client to deal with data manipulation features. HBase also unfolds an API for data definition such as operations related to HBase tables, column family and so on. Table creation in HBase implicitly requires the table schema definition and the schemas for all contained column families. Let's start with the data definition API.

The data definition API

In HBase, all data is grouped into tables. The important things required to define a table are column families. The `HTableDescriptor` class contains the details about an HBase table such as the descriptors of all the column families, type of the table that is catalog table or `hbase:meta`. It also defines whether the table is read-only or not, the maximum size of MemStore, when the region split should occur, the registered coprocessors, and so on. The following is the list of constructors available for the `HTableDescriptor` class:

HTableDescriptor(HTableDescriptor desc)

The preceding constructor takes the existing descriptor as a parameter and clones it to construct the new table descriptor.

HTableDescriptor(TableName name)

The preceding constructor takes the `TableName` object to construct the table descriptor.

HTableDescriptor(TableName name, HColumnDescriptor[] families)

HTableDescriptor(TableName name, HColumnDescriptor[] families, Map<Immuta bleBytesWritable,ImmutableBytesWritable> values)

The preceding two protected constructors are used internally to create table descriptors for catalog table and `hbase:meta`. Once table descriptor objects are created, the descriptor provides getters and setters to set different options for the table.

Table name methods

Getters methods provided to access the name of the table as either `byte[]` or `String` are as follows:

```
byte[] getName();
String getNameAsString();
```

Column family methods

The `HTableDescriptor` class which is a class of `TableDescriptor`, provides methods to specify the column families to be used with the table, and they are as follows:

- `void addFamily(HColumnDescriptor family)`: This adds a column family to the table description

- `boolean hasFamily(byte[] c)`: This checks whether the table descriptor contains the given column family

- `HColumnDescriptor[] getColumnFamilies()`: This returns an array of the `HColumnDescriptor` object for the column families of the table

- `HColumnDescriptor getFamily(byte[] column)`: This returns the `HColumnDescriptor` object for a specific column family name specified as the parameter

- `HColumnDescriptor removeFamily(byte[] column)`: This removes the `HColumnDescriptor` object from the table description for the column family name specified by the parameter

Other methods

The `HTableDescriptor` class also provides other useful methods to specify the maximum size for a region within the table to get the MemStore size and so on. The following is the list of some important methods:

```
long getMaxFileSize();
void setMaxFileSize(long maxFileSize);
```

The getter and setter is set for the maximum size up to which a region can grow, the maximum size helps the system to split regions when they reach the maximum configured size.

The table descriptor also provides methods to specify the tables as read only (by default, all tables are write enabled). Read-only tables cannot be modified and can only be used to access the data. The `boolean isReadOnly()` option checks whether the `read-only` flag is set for the table. The void `setReadOnly(boolean readOnly)` option sets the table and all the columns in it as read only.

As discussed earlier, the in-memory store is used to buffer the values before writing them to disk. We can set the buffer size for the in-memory store using the following methods:

```
long getMemStoreFlushSize();
```

```
void setMemStoreFlushSize(long memstoreFlushSize);
```

The getter and setter is set for the size of the in-memory store; once this in-memory store is completely filled, the flush operation to write the in-memory data to disk is triggered. The default size of the in-memory store is 64 MB.

Like the `HTableDescriptor` class, we also have the `HColumnDescriptor` class that provides methods to specify different settings at the column family level. Using these methods, a client can create any number of columns at run time where columns are accessed as a combination of the column family name and the column qualifier (or column key). The `HTableDescriptor` class provides a number of constructors, the following are some of the non deprecated ones:

- `HColumnDescriptor(byte[] familyName)`: This constructs a column descriptor object by passing the family name as a `byte[]` parameter
- `HColumnDescriptor(String familyName)`: This constructs a column descriptor object by passing the family name as a string parameter

Some of the useful methods defined in the `HColumnDescriptor` class are as follows:

```
byte[] getName()
```
```
String getNameAsString()
```

The preceding command shows a different getter for getting the column family name.

```
int getMaxVersions()
```
```
HColumnDescriptor setMaxVersions(int maxVersions)
```

The preceding command shows different getter and setter methods for the maximum number of versions for a column value (default value 3).

The following are the list of getter and setter methods to handle compression and compaction:

```
Compression.Algorithm getCompression();

Compression.Algorithm getCompressionType();

void setCompressionType(Compression.Algorithm type);

Compression.Algorithm getCompactionCompression();

Compression.Algorithm  getCompactionCompressionType();

void setCompactionCompressionType (Compression.Algorithm type);

Compression.Algorithm getCompactionCompression();

Compression.Algorithm getCompactionCompression();

Compression.Algorithm getCompactionCompressionType();

void setCompactionCompressionType (Compression.Algorithm type);
```

In HBase, all files are divided into a smaller number of blocks that are loaded during a `get` or `scan` operation. The `HColumnDescriptor` class defines the methods to set the block size where the default value is 64 KB:

```
int getBlocksize();

HColumnDescriptor setBlocksize(int s);
```

The preceding command shows the getter and setter methods for the block size of the storefile/HFile for a column family.

Similar to block size, the `HColumnDescriptor` class also defines methods to enable/disable the in-memory block cache, which is used to avoid the frequent disk I/O. The following methods of an API can be used to change this flag:

- `boolean isBlockCacheEnabled()`: This returns true if caching of the HFile data type blocks is enabled

- `void setBlockCacheEnabled(boolean blockCacheEnabled)`: This enables caching for HFile data type blocks

Enabling block cache does not guarantee the persistence of values of the column family in-memory. By default, the in-memory flag is `false` and can be modified using the following methods:

- `boolean isInMemory()`: This returns `true` if the `HRegionServer` level caching is enabled for all values of the column family.

- `HColumnDescriptor setInMemory(boolean inMemory)`: This enables the `HRegionServer` level in-memory caching for the values of the column family. It returns the `"this"` instance.

The HBaseAdmin API

Just like the data definition API or data manipulation with the client API, HBase also provides the API for handling administrative tasks. The `HBaseAdmin` class provides an interface to manage HBase database table metadata and general administrative functions. Before using the administrative API, an instance of the `HBaseAdmin` class needs to be created as follows:

HBaseAdmin(org.apache.hadoop.conf.Configurationconf)

The existing configuration instance is passed as a parameter that provides details about the cluster using the ZooKeeper quorum. The `HBaseAdmin` class unfolds the following methods for administrative operations:

- `boolean isMasterRunning()`: This returns true if the master server is running; otherwise, it throws an exception.

- `HConnection getConnection()`: This returns a connection instance to the HBase master.

- `Configuration getConfiguration()`: This returns the configuration used by the current instance. The HBaseAdmin instance can also be used to modify the configuration for a running HBaseAdmin instance.

- `close()`: This closes all resources kept by the current HBaseAdmin instance. This includes the connection to the remote servers.

Once the connection is established, HBase table-related calls can be used to create a table as follows:

void createTable(HTableDescriptor desc)

The preceding command creates a new table synchronously by taking the `HTableDescriptor` instance as a parameter.

void createTable(HTableDescriptor desc, byte[] startKey,byte[] endKey, int numRegions)

The preceding command creates a new table with the specified number of regions. The start key specified will become the end key of the first region of the table, and the end key specified will become the start key of the last region of the table (the first region has a null start key and the last region has a null end key).

void createTable(HTableDescriptor desc, byte[] [] splitKeys)

This creates a new table with an initial set of empty regions defined by the specified split keys synchronously. The total number of regions created will be the number of split keys plus one.

void createTableAsync(HTableDescriptor desc, byte[] [] splitKeys)

This creates a new table but does not block and wait for it to come online asynchronously.

Once you have created a table, the following helper functions can be used for table related operations:

```
boolean tableExists(String tableName)
boolean tableExists(byte[] tableName)
```

The preceding methods check the existence of a table:

The `HTableDescriptor[] listTables()` command lists all the user space tables, in other words, scans the `hbase:meta` table.

The `HTableDescriptor getTableDescriptor(byte[] tableName)` command returns the instance of the `HTableDescriptor` class for the table.

```
void deleteTable(String tableName)
void deleteTable(byte[] tableName)
deleteTable(TableName tableName)
deleteTables(String regex)
deleteTables(Pattern pattern)
```

The preceding method deletes the table, takes the table name as a string or byte array, and removes the table from the servers with all data deleted.

Before deletion, tables need to be disabled first. The disabling operation notifies every region server to flush any uncommitted data to the disk, closes the regions, and updates the `hbase:meta` table so that no region of a targeted table gets deployed to any servers. Disabling of a table can be performed using the following methods:

```
void disableTable(String tableName)
void disableTable(byte[] tableName)
disableTable(TableName tableName)
void disableTableAsync(String tableName)
void disableTableAsync(byte[] tableName)
disableTableAsync(TableName tableName)
disableTables(Pattern pattern)
```

Apart from table operation the `HBaseAdmin` class also exposes operations related to clusters such as checking the status of the cluster or performing tasks on tables and/or regions.

The static void `checkHBaseAvailable(Configuration conf)` command checks whether remote HBase is running and available for the client, based on the configuration passed as the parameter and throws an exception if not. The following are the methods for cluster operations:

```
closeRegion(byte[] regionname, String serverName)
```

```
closeRegion(ServerName sn, HRegionInfo hri)
```

```
closeRegion(String regionname, String serverName)
```

```
closeRegionWithEncodedRegionName(String encodedRegionName, String serverName)
```

The preceding methods are used to close regions that have been deployed to region servers. An `Enable` table has all regions enabled that need to be closed and undeployed.

```
void flush(String tableNameOrRegionName)
```

```
void flush(byte[] tableNameOrRegionName)
```

The preceding methods update the region or table with unflushed data accumulated in the MemStore instances of the region on a region server. The client application can also use the preceding methods synchronously to flush such pending records to disk before they are implicitly written.

```
void compact(String tableNameOrRegionName)
```

```
compact(String tableOrRegionName, String columnFamily)
```

```
void compact(byte[] tableNameOrRegionName)
```

```
compact(byte[] tableNameOrRegionName, byte[] columnFamily)
```

Similar to the previous operations, using the preceding methods' compaction operation can also be called by the client asynchronously, as compactions usually take a long time to complete. The compaction operation queues the table or region for compaction, which is executed in the background by the server hosting the named region, or by all servers hosting any region of the given table:

```
void split(String tableNameOrRegionName)
```

```
void split(byte[] tableNameOrRegionName)
```

```
void split(String tableNameOrRegionName, String splitPoint)
```

```
void split(byte[] tableNameOrRegionName, byte[] splitPoint)
```

The preceding methods cause the table or region to split alike. In the case of a table, it iterates over all regions of that table and implicitly invokes the split command on each of them.

```
setBalancerRunning(boolean on, boolean synchronous)
Boolean boolean balancer()
```

The first method in the preceding command switches the region balancer on or off and for the enabled balancer. A call to the `balancer()` method will start the process of balancing regions across the servers.

```
void shutdown()
void stopMaster() {
void stopRegionServer(String hostnamePort)
```

The preceding command calls either shuts down the entire cluster, stops the master server, or stops a particular region server alone. Once invoked, the affected servers will be stopped and there is no way to revert the process.

The `HBaseAdmin.getClusterStatus()` command returns the `ClusterStatus` instance, containing all the information about the master server and current state of the cluster. The following methods are available within the `ClusterStatus` class to access the different information available within the cluster:

- `int getServersSize()`: This returns the number of live region servers known to the master server.
- `Collection<ServerName>getServers()`: This returns the list of live servers. Server names in the collection are the ServerName instances that contain the hostname, RPC port, and start code.
- `int getDeadServers()`: This returns the number of servers listed as dead.
- `Collection<ServerName>getDeadServerNames()`: This returns the list of dead servers. Server names in the collection are ServerName instances that contain the hostname, RPC port, and start code.
- `double getAverageLoad()`: This returns the total average number of regions per region server.

- `int getRegionsCount()`: This returns the total number of regions in the cluster.

- `int getRequestsCount()`: This returns the current number of requests across all regions' servers in the cluster.

- `String getHBaseVersion()`: This returns the HBase version identification string.

- `byte getVersion()`: This returns the version of the ClusterStatus instance used during the serialization process of sending an instance over RPC.

- `String getClusterId()`: This returns the unique identifier for the cluster. This is the UUID generated when HBase starts with an empty storage directory. It is stored in hbase.id under the root directory.

- `Map<String, RegionState>getRegionsInTransition()`: This returns the map of all regions currently in transition, for example, it is moved, assigned, or unassigned.

 Refer to the API documentation for HBase at `https://hbase.apache.org/apidocs/index.html`.

Summary

In this chapter, we have learned about the advanced topics such as counters and coprocessors in detail. We have also looked into the details of the advanced API provided by HBase for data definition and HBase administration.

In the next chapter, we will discuss the various clients available for HBase such as REST client, Thrift client, Kundera, and so on.

6
HBase Clients

In the previous chapter, we covered the HBase API and its usage for various features. Apart from the API, there are different flavors of clients that can be used with different programming languages to access HBase. This chapter is completely focused on the different clients we can use to access the HBase cluster. We will cover the following topics:

- The HBase shell
- Kundera – the object mapper
- The REST client
- The Thrift client
- The Hadoop ecosystem client

Let's start with the HBase shell first.

The HBase shell

The easiest way to access HBase is using the command-line interface called the HBase shell. The HBase shell is based on the Java Virtual Machine-based implementation of Ruby (JRuby) and can be used to connect to local or remote servers for interaction. It also provides both client and administrative operations. The HBase shell, the default HBase tool that comes with the HBase installation, can be launched as follows:

```
$HBASE_HOME/bin/hbase shell
HBase Shell; enter 'help<RETURN>' for list of supported commands.
Type "exit<RETURN>" to leave the HBase Shell
Version 0.96.2-hadoop2, r1581096, Mon Mar 24 16:03:18 PDT 2014
hbase(main):001:0>
```

To exit from the HBase shell, the exit or quit command is used as follows:

```
hbase(main):002:0> quit
```

Once the HBase shell is started, you can type in help, and then, click on **Return** to get the help text and the list of all the commands, as shown in the following screenshot:

```
hbase(main):001:0> help
HBase Shell, version 0.96.2-hadoop2, r1581096, Mon Mar 24 16:03:18 PDT 2014
Type 'help "COMMAND"', (e.g. 'help "get"' -- the quotes are necessary) for hel
p on a specific command.
Commands are grouped. Type 'help "COMMAND_GROUP"', (e.g. 'help "general"') for
 help on a command group.

COMMAND GROUPS:
  Group name: general
  Commands: status, table_help, version, whoami

  Group name: ddl
  Commands: alter, alter_async, alter_status, create, describe, disable, disab
le_all, drop, drop_all, enable, enable_all, exists, get_table, is_disabled, is
_enabled, list, show_filters
```

Let's take a look at the various commands available with the HBase shell.

Data definition commands

The following table shows the list of frequently used data definition commands that can be used from the HBase shell:

Command	Description
create	Creates a new table
alter	Modifies an existing table schema
disable	Disables a table
drop	Drops a table
enable	Enables a table
describe	Prints the table descriptor
exists	Checks whether a table exists
list	Returns a list of all user tables

Data manipulation commands

The following table shows the list of frequently used data manipulation commands that can be used from the HBase shell:

Command	Description
put	Stores a cell
scan	Scans a range of rows
get	Retrieves a cell
truncate	Truncates a table; this command is a combination of the disable and drop commands
delete	Deletes a cell
deleteall	Deletes an entire family or row
count	Counts the rows in a table
incr	Increments a counter

Data-handling tools

The following table shows the list of frequently used data-handling administrative tools that can be used from the HBase shell:

Command	Description
assign	Assigns a region to a server
balancer	Starts the balancer
compact	Starts the asynchronous compaction of a region or table
flush	Starts the asynchronous flush of a region or table
move	Moves a region to a different region server
split	Splits a region or table

For detailed help on any command, type `help '<command>'`, as shown in the following command:

```
hbase(main):003:0> help 'create'
```

```
Creates a table. Pass a table name, and a set of column family
specifications (at least one), and, optionally, table configuration.
Column specification can be a simple string (name), or a dictionary
(dictionaries are described below in main help output), necessarily
including NAME attribute. Examples:
```

Create a table with namespace=ns1 and table qualifier=t1

```
hbase> create 'ns1:t1', {NAME => 'f1', VERSIONS => 5}
```

Create a table with namespace=default and table qualifier=t1

```
hbase> create 't1', {NAME => 'f1'}, {NAME => 'f2'}, {NAME => 'f3'}
hbase> # The above in shorthand would be the following:
hbase> create 't1', 'f1', 'f2', 'f3'
hbase> create 't1', {NAME => 'f1', VERSIONS => 1, TTL => 2592000,
BLOCKCACHE => true}
hbase> create 't1', {NAME => 'f1', CONFIGURATION => {'hbase.hstore.
blockingStoreFiles' => '10'}}
```

Table configuration options can be put at the end, as shown in the following example:

```
hbase> create 'ns1:t1', 'f1', SPLITS => ['10', '20', '30', '40']
hbase> create 't1', 'f1', SPLITS => ['10', '20', '30', '40']
hbase> create 't1', 'f1', SPLITS_FILE => 'splits.txt', OWNER =>
'johndoe'
hbase> create 't1', {NAME => 'f1', VERSIONS => 5}, METADATA => {
'mykey' => 'myvalue' }
hbase> # Optionally pre-split the table into NUMREGIONS, using
hbase> # SPLITALGO ("HexStringSplit", "UniformSplit" or classname)
hbase> create 't1', 'f1', {NUMREGIONS => 15, SPLITALGO =>
'HexStringSplit'}
hbase> create 't1', 'f1', {NUMREGIONS => 15, SPLITALGO =>
'HexStringSplit', CONFIGURATION => {'hbase.hregion.scan.
loadColumnFamiliesOnDemand' => 'true'}}
```

You can also keep a reference to the created table:

```
hbase> t1 = create 't1', 'f1'
```

This gives you a reference to the table named 't1', on which you can then call methods.

Kundera – object mapper

In order to start using HBase in your Java application with minimal learning, you can use one of the popular open source API named Kundera, which is a JPA 2.1 compliant object mapper. Kundera is a polyglot object mapper for NoSQL, as well as RDBMS data stores. It is a single high-level Java API that supports eight NoSQL data stores. The idea behind Kundera is to make working with NoSQL databases drop-dead simple and fun. Kundera provides the following qualities:

- A robust querying system
- Easy object/relation mapping
- Support for secondary level caching and event-based data handling
- Optimized data store persistence
- Connection pooling and Lucene-based indexing

Kundera supports cross-datastore persistence, that is, it supports polyglot persistence between supported NoSQL datastores and RDBMS. This means you can store and fetch related entities in different datastores using a single method call. It manages transactions beautifully and supports both **Entity Transaction** and **Java Transaction API (JTA)**. The following are the three possible ways to start using Kundera:

- Using Kundera Binaries: Kundera binaries are available at `https://oss.sonatype.org/content/repositories/releases/com/impetus/kundera/`.

- Using as a Maven dependency: If you have a Maven project, then simply add the following repository and dependency into your project's `pom.xml` file to include Kundera in your project:

```
<repositories>
  <repository>
    <id>sonatype-nexus</id>
    <name>Kundera Public Repository</name>
    <url>https://oss.sonatype.org/content/repositories/
releases</url>
    <releases>
```

```
      <enabled>true</enabled>
    </releases>
    <snapshots>
      <enabled>false</enabled>
    </snapshots>
  </repository>
  <repository>
    <id>kundera-missing</id>
    <name>Kundera Public Missing Resources Repository</name>
  <url>http://kundera.googlecode.com/svn/maven2/maven-missing-
resources</url>
    <releases>
      <enabled>true</enabled>
    </releases>
    <snapshots>
      <enabled>true</enabled>
    </snapshots>
  </repository>
</repositories>
    <dependency>
        <groupId>com.impetus.kundera.client</groupId>
        <artifactId>kundera-hbase</artifactId>
        <version>${kundera.version}</version>
    </dependency>
```

- Building from source: you can build Kundera from source as well. In order to do so, you first need to download the source code. It's a Maven-based project; so, using Maven, you can build each module of Kundera. To build a specific module (for example, src). you need to execute the following command:

```
mvn clean install -Dfile src/pom.xml
```

Once the Kundera binaries are available using either of the preceding three ways, include binaries (kundera-hbase.jar) in the classpath project to use it with HBase.

CRUD using Kundera

It is very easy to perform CRUD operations using Kundera. To perform CRUD operations, we need to have an instance of `EntityManager`. Obtaining an `EntityManager` instance consists of two steps. First, we need to obtain an instance of `EntityManagerFactory`, and then, we can use this factory instance to get an `EntityManager` instance. JPA requires the definition of a persistence-unit in an XML file in order to create an `EntityManagerFactory` instance, as follows:

```
EntityManagerFactory emf = Persistence.createEntityManagerFactory("hba
se_pu");

EntityManager em = emf.createEntityManager();
```

A sample persistence-unit is as follows:

```
<persistence-unit name="hbase_pu">

  <provider>com.impetus.kundera.KunderaPersistence</provider>

    <properties>

    <property name="kundera.nodes" value="localhost" />

    <property name="kundera.port" value="2181" />

    <property name="kundera.keyspace" value="KunderaExample" />

    <property name="kundera.dialect" value="hbase" />

    <property name="kundera.client.lookup.class" value="com.impetus.
client.hbase.HBaseClientFactory" />

  </properties>

</persistence-unit>
```

Now, let's take an example to explore the implementation of CRUD operations using Kundera. An organization wants to maintain their employee records with some attributes such as name, address, date of joining, and department. In order to map the data columns, you need to create equivalent Java entity objects.

The following code shows the implementation of an employee entity as `Employee.java`:

```
@Entity
@Table(name = "EMPLOYEE")
public class Employee {

  @Id
  private String employeeId;

  @Column
  private String employeeName;

  @Column
  private String address;

  @Column
  private String department;

  public Employee() {
    // Default constructor.
  }

  // getters and setters.
}
```

Once the employee entity is created, implement the **create, read, update and delete (CRUD)** operations to be performed:

```
private static EntityManagerFactory emf = Persistence
  .createEntityManagerFactory("hbaseTest");
private static EntityManager em = emf.createEntityManager();
```

The CRUD operation is explained as follows:

- **The create operation**: The following code shows the creation of an employee record:

```
Employee employee = new Employee();
employee.setEmployeeId("1");
employee.setEmployeeName("John");
employee.setAddress("Atlanta");
employee.setDepartment("R&D Labs");

// persist employee record.
em.persist(employee);
```

Once the employee record is created, run the scan command to view the record stored, as shown in the following screenshot:

```
kuldeep@localhost:/usr/local/hbase-0.96.1.1-hadoop2/bin$ ./hbase shell
2014-07-28 23:15:21,027 INFO  [main] Configuration.deprecation: hadoop.native.lib is deprecated. Instead, use io.native.lib.avail
able
HBase Shell; enter 'help<RETURN>' for list of supported commands.
Type "exit<RETURN>" to leave the HBase Shell
Version 0.96.1.1-hadoop2, rUnknown, Tue Dec 17 12:22:12 PST 2013

hbase(main):001:0> list
TABLE
2014-07-28 23:16:00,301 WARN  [main] util.NativeCodeLoader: Unable to load native-hadoop library for your platform... using built
in-java classes where applicable
KunderaExamples
1 row(s) in 4.8710 seconds

=> ["KunderaExamples"]
hbase(main):002:0> scan 'KunderaExamples'
ROW                          COLUMN+CELL
 1                           column=EMPLOYEE:address, timestamp=1406569552873, value=sector-12, noida
 1                           column=EMPLOYEE:department, timestamp=1406569552873, value=R&D Labs
 1                           column=EMPLOYEE:employeeName, timestamp=1406569552873, value=Kuldeep
1 row(s) in 0.0540 seconds

hbase(main):003:0>
```

- **The read operation**: The following code shows the reading of the employee record:

```
System.out.println("Finding employee record operation.");

// Find persisted employee record.
Employee foundEmployee = em.find(Employee.class, "1");

System.out.println(foundEmployee.getEmployeeId());
System.out.println(foundEmployee.getEmployeeName());
System.out.println(foundEmployee.getAddress());
System.out.println(foundEmployee.getDepartment());
```

- **The update operation**: The following code shows the update process of the employee record:

```
// update employee record.
System.out.println("Updating existing employee record.");

foundEmployee.setAddress("New York");
  em.merge(foundEmployee);

System.out.println("Finding employee post merge operation.");

// Find updated employee record.
Employee updatedEmployee = em.find(Employee.class, "1");

System.out.println(updatedEmployee.getEmployeeId());
System.out.println(updatedEmployee.getEmployeeName());
System.out.println(updatedEmployee.getAddress());
System.out.println(updatedEmployee.getDepartment());
```

Once the employee record is updated, run the `scan` command to verify the record updation, as shown in the following screenshot:

```
kuldeep@localhost:/usr/local/hbase-0.96.1.1-hadoop2/bin$ ./hbase shell
2014-07-28 23:15:21,027 INFO  [main] Configuration.deprecation: hadoop.native.lib is deprecated. Instead, use io.native.lib.avail
able
HBase Shell; enter 'help<RETURN>' for list of supported commands.
Type "exit<RETURN>" to leave the HBase Shell
Version 0.96.1.1-hadoop2, rUnknown, Tue Dec 17 12:22:12 PST 2013

hbase(main):001:0> list
TABLE
2014-07-28 23:16:00,301 WARN  [main] util.NativeCodeLoader: Unable to load native-hadoop library for your platform... using built
in-java classes where applicable
KunderaExamples
1 row(s) in 4.8710 seconds

=> ["KunderaExamples"]
hbase(main):002:0> scan 'KunderaExamples'
ROW                         COLUMN+CELL
 1                          column=EMPLOYEE:address, timestamp=1406569552873, value=sector-12, noida
 1                          column=EMPLOYEE:department, timestamp=1406569552873, value=R&D Labs
 1                          column=EMPLOYEE:employeeName, timestamp=1406569552873, value=Kuldeep
1 row(s) in 0.0540 seconds

hbase(main):003:0> scan 'KunderaExamples'
ROW                         COLUMN+CELL
 1                          column=EMPLOYEE:address, timestamp=1406569596672, value=sector-11, noida
 1                          column=EMPLOYEE:department, timestamp=1406569596672, value=R&D Labs
 1                          column=EMPLOYEE:employeeName, timestamp=1406569596672, value=Kuldeep
1 row(s) in 0.0280 seconds

hbase(main):004:0>
```

- The delete operation: The following code shows the deletion of the employee record:

```
// delete employee record.
em.remove(foundEmployee);

// Find deleted employee record, it should be null.
Employee deletedEmployee = em.find(Employee.class, "1");

System.out.println("After deletion employee object is"
        + deletedEmployee);
// close em instance.
em.close();

// close emf instance.
emf.close();
```

Once the employee record is deleted, run the scan command to verify the successful record deletion, as shown in the following screenshot:

```
2014-07-28 23:15:21,027 INFO  [main] Configuration.deprecation: hadoop.native.lib is deprecated. Instead, use io.native.lib.avail
able
HBase Shell; enter 'help<RETURN>' for list of supported commands.
Type "exit<RETURN>" to leave the HBase Shell
Version 0.96.1.1-hadoop2, rUnknown, Tue Dec 17 12:22:12 PST 2013

hbase(main):001:0> list
TABLE
2014-07-28 23:16:00,301 WARN  [main] util.NativeCodeLoader: Unable to load native-hadoop library for your platform... using built
in-java classes where applicable
KunderaExamples
1 row(s) in 4.8710 seconds

=> ["KunderaExamples"]
hbase(main):002:0> scan 'KunderaExamples'
ROW                          COLUMN+CELL
 1                           column=EMPLOYEE:address, timestamp=1406569552873, value=sector-12, noida
 1                           column=EMPLOYEE:department, timestamp=1406569552873, value=R&D Labs
 1                           column=EMPLOYEE:employeeName, timestamp=1406569552873, value=Kuldeep
1 row(s) in 0.0540 seconds

hbase(main):003:0> scan 'KunderaExamples'
ROW                          COLUMN+CELL
 1                           column=EMPLOYEE:address, timestamp=1406569596672, value=sector-11, noida
 1                           column=EMPLOYEE:department, timestamp=1406569596672, value=R&D Labs
 1                           column=EMPLOYEE:employeeName, timestamp=1406569596672, value=Kuldeep
1 row(s) in 0.0280 seconds

hbase(main):004:0> scan 'KunderaExamples'
ROW                          COLUMN+CELL
0 row(s) in 0.0150 seconds

hbase(main):005:0>
```

Query HBase using Kundera

In order to query HBase using Kundera, you first need to create a `Query` instance using `EntityManager` and then call the `getResultList()` method of the `query` class to get a list of results. The following code shows a few examples of querying HBase using Kundera:

```
//Select without where cause 1.e. Select all.
String queryString = "Select e from Employee e";
Query query = em.createQuery(queryString);
List<Employee> employees = query.getResultList();

System.out.println(employees.size());

employee = employees.get(0);

System.out.println(employee.getEmployeeId());
System.out.println(employee.getEmployeeName());
System.out.println(employee.getAddress());
System.out.println(employee.getDepartment());

// Select Query with constraints on employee name.
queryString = "Select e from Employee e where e.employeeName=John";
query = em.createQuery(queryString);
employees = query.getResultList();

System.out.println(employees.size());
employee = employees.get(0);

System.out.println(employee.getEmployeeId());
System.out.println(employee.getEmployeeName());
System.out.println(employee.getAddress());
System.out.println(employee.getDepartment());

// Select specific columns only.
queryString = "Select e.employeeName, e.address from Employee e";
query = em.createQuery(queryString);
employees = query.getResultList();

System.out.println(employees.size());
employee = employees.get(0);
```

```
System.out.println(employee.getEmployeeId());
System.out.println(employee.getEmployeeName());
System.out.println(employee.getAddress());
System.out.println(employee.getDepartment());
```

Using filters within query

To start using filters with Kundera, perform the following steps:

1. Create the `EntityManager` instance and use the `getDelegate` method to get the map of clients.

2. Fetch the client from the map of clients, specific to your persistence-unit.

3. Finally, create a `Filter` object of whichever filter you want to use and set it into the HbaseClient object:

```
Map<String, Client> clients = (Map<String, Client>)
em.getDelegate();
  HBaseClient client = (HBaseClient) clients.get("hbaseTest");
  Filter prefixFilter = new PrefixFilter(Bytes.toBytes("1"));
  client.setFilter(prefixFilter);
```

The following code shows a few examples using the filter while querying HBase using Kundera:

```
String queryString = "Select e from Employee e";
Query query = em.createQuery(queryString);
List<Employee> employees = query.getResultList();

System.out.println(employees.size());

employee = employees.get(0);

System.out.println(employee.getEmployeeId());
System.out.println(employee.getEmployeeName());
System.out.println(employee.getAddress());
System.out.println(employee.getDepartment());

Filter keyOnlyFilter = new KeyOnlyFilter();
```

```
// Only row key will be fetched.
client.setFilter(keyOnlyFilter);
queryString = "Select e from Employee e";
query = em.createQuery(queryString);
employees = query.getResultList();

System.out.println(employees.size());

employee = employees.get(0);

System.out.println(employee.getEmployeeId());
System.out.println(employee.getEmployeeName());

System.out.println(employee.getAddress());
System.out.println(employee.getDepartment());
```

You can start using HBase in your project using Kundera very easily. A few highlighting features of Kundera that makes working with HBase simple are as follows:

- It serves as a JPA compliant solution. JPA is a very popular Java API specification for RDBMS for a long period of time.

- It allows you to focus on the domain model and forget the complexity of NoSQL by enabling you to perform operations and query data using the common high-level API.

- It enables switching across data stores using the same code by simply changing configurations.

REST clients

HBase has a close relationship with Java. In the Java world, REST is a way to interact with objects over the Web. HBase provides the REST service that runs as a separate process and communicates with HBase. This REST service uses the same client API to access HBase.

Getting started

For a REST-based client to make a connection to an HBase cluster, first start the REST server on the HBase Master as follows:

```
[root@localhost bin]# hbase rest

...

usage: bin/hbase rest start [--infoport <arg>] [-p <arg>] [-ro]
    --infoport <arg>    Port for web UI
 -p,--port <arg>        Port to bind to [default: 8080]
 -ro,--readonly         Respond only to GET HTTP method requests [default:
                        false]
```

To run the REST server as a daemon, execute the following command:

```
bin/hbase-daemon.sh start|stop rest [--infoport <port>] [-p <port>] [-ro]
```

For example, launch the REST service, listening on port 9999 using the following command:

```
[root@localhost bin]#  hbase rest start -p 9999


Or as daemon service:


[root@localhost bin]# ./hbase-daemon.sh start rest -p 9999


Once the service is started, curl# command can be used to verify the
service status:


[root@localhost bin]# curl http://localhost:9999/
firsttable
tab2
```

The preceding command returns the list of tables in HBase. To check the REST server version and the JVM and OS details of the machine it is running on, use the following command:

```
[root@localhost bin]# curl http://localhost:9999/version
rest 0.0.2 [JVM: Oracle Corporation 1.7.0_45-24.45-b08] [OS: Linux
2.6.32-358.23.2.el6.x86_64 amd64] [Server: jetty/6.1.26] [Jersey: 1.8]
```

The REST service supports multiple-type response formats such as plain, XML, JSON, protocol buffer, and binary. These formats vary based on the value of the content type request header. The different possible values for the content-type are `text/plain`, `text/xml`, `application/json`, `application/x-protobuf`, and `application/octet-stream`. The following are examples of how to use each content type.

The plain format

The following is an example of how to use the plain format:

```
[root@localhost bin]# curl -H "Accept: text/plain" http://localhost:9999/
version

rest 0.0.2 [JVM: Oracle Corporation 1.7.0_45-24.45-b08] [OS: Linux
2.6.32-358.23.2.el6.x86_64 amd64] [Server: jetty/6.1.26] [Jersey: 1.8]
```

The XML format

The following is an example of how to use the XML format:

```
[root@localhost bin]# curl -H "Accept: text/xml" http://localhost:9999/
version
<?xml version="1.0" encoding="UTF-8" standalone="yes"?><Version
JVM="Oracle Corporation 1.7.0_45-24.45-b08" Jersey="1.8" OS="Linux
2.6.32-358.23.2.el6.x86_64 amd64" REST="0.0.2" Server="jetty/6.1.26"/>
```

The JSON format (defined as a key-value pair)

The following is an example of how to use the JSON format:

```
[root@localhost bin]# curl -H "Accept: application/json" http://
localhost:9999/version
{"REST":"0.0.2","JVM":"Oracle Corporation 1.7.0_45-24.45-b08","OS":"Linux
2.6.32-358.23.2.el6.x86_64 amd64","Server":"jetty/6.1.26","Jersey":"1.8
```

The protocol buffer format and binary decoders are primarily used to handle data in the binary format and binary decoders are required if data conversion is required.

The REST Java client

The Java client API for the REST server is located in the `org.apache.hadoop.hbase.rest.client` package. The following is the sample Java client for REST:

```
package com.ch6;

import org.apache.hadoop.hbase.client.Get;
import org.apache.hadoop.hbase.client.Result;
import org.apache.hadoop.hbase.client.ResultScanner;
import org.apache.hadoop.hbase.client.Scan;
import org.apache.hadoop.hbase.rest.client.Client;
import org.apache.hadoop.hbase.rest.client.Cluster;
import org.apache.hadoop.hbase.rest.client.RemoteHTable;
import org.apache.hadoop.hbase.util.Bytes;

public class HBaseRESTCLient {

  private static RemoteHTable table;

  public static void main(String[] args) throws Exception {
    Cluster hbaseCluster = new Cluster();
    hbaseCluster.add("localhost", 9999);
    // Create Rest client instance and get the connection
Client restClient = new Client(hbaseCluster);
    table = new RemoteHTable(restClient, "tab1");

    Get get = new Get(Bytes.toBytes("row-3"));
get.addColumn(Bytes.toBytes("cf1"), Bytes.toBytes("greet"));

Result result1 = table.get(get);
    System.out.println("Get Results - " + result1);

    Scan scan = new Scan();
    scan.setStartRow(Bytes.toBytes("row-10"));
    scan.setStopRow(Bytes.toBytes("row-15"));
    scan.addColumn(Bytes.toBytes("cf1"), Bytes.toBytes("pie"));
```

```
    ResultScanner scanner = table.getScanner(scan);
    System.out.println("Scan Results - ");


    for (Result result2 : scanner) {
System.out.println("row[" + Bytes.toString(result2.getRow())
        + "]: " + result2);
    }
  }
}
```

The Thrift client

The Apache Thrift software framework is used for cross-language services development. It is bundled with a code generation engine to build services that work seamlessly between C++, Java, Python, PHP, Ruby, Erlang, Perl, JavaScript, Node.js, Smalltalk, OCaml, Delphi, and other languages.

 Get started with the Apache Thrift installation and working example at https://thrift.apache.org/.

After the Thrift compiler is installed, create a `thrift` file. This file is an **interface definition (ID)** made up of Thrift types and services. The services defined in the ID file are implemented by the server and are called by any clients. The Thrift compiler is used to convert the `thrift` File into source code which is used by the different client libraries and the server.

Getting started

For a Thrift-based client to make a connection to a HBase cluster, first start the Thrift server on the HBase Master as follows:

```
[root@localhost bin]# hbase thrift

usage: Thrift [-b <arg>] [-c] [-f] [-h] [-hsha | -nonblocking |
-threadedselector | -threadpool] [--infoport <arg>] [-k <arg>] [-m <arg>]
[-p <arg>] [-q <arg>]    [-w <arg>]
 -b,--bind <arg>          Address to bind the Thrift server to.
[default:

                         0.0.0.0]
```

`-c,--compact`	Use the compact protocol
`-f,--framed`	Use framed transport
`-h,--help`	Print help information
`-hsha`	Use the THsHaServer This implies the framed transport.
`--infoport <arg>`	Port for web UI
`-k,--keepAliveSec <arg>`	The amount of time in seconds to keep a thread alive when idle in TBoundedThreadPoolServer
`-m,--minWorkers <arg>`	The minimum number of worker threads for TBoundedThreadPoolServer
`-nonblocking`	Use the TNonblockingServer This implies the framed transport.
`-p,--port <arg>`	Port to bind to [default: 9090]
`-q,--queue <arg>`	The maximum number of queued requests in TBoundedThreadPoolServer
`-threadedselector`	Use the TThreadedSelectorServer This implies the framed transport.
`-threadpool`	Use the TBoundedThreadPoolServerThis is the default.
`-w,--workers <arg>`	The maximum number of worker threads for TBoundedThreadPoolServer

To start the Thrift server, run `bin/hbase-daemon.sh start thrift`. To shut down the Thrift server, run `bin/hbase-daemon.sh stop thrift` or send a kill signal to the Thrift server pid. For example, launch the Thrift service, listening on port 9999 using:

```
[root@localhost bin]#  hbase thrift start -p 9999
```

Otherwise, as a daemon service, use the following command:

```
[root@localhost bin]#  ./hbase-daemon.sh start thrift -p 9999
```

The Thrift server provides all the operations required to work with HBase tables. The HBase default package comes with the Thrift schema file and an example client for many programming languages such as C++, PHP, Perl, Protobuf, Ruby, Python, and so on. The following is a Python example to store and retrieve the data from HBase:

```
#import thrift libraries
#! /usr/bin/env python
```

```python
import sys
import os
import time

from thrift.transport import TTransport
from thrift.transport import TSocket
from thrift.transport import THttpClient
from thrift.protocol import TBinaryProtocol

from hbase import THBaseService
from hbase.ttypes import *

# Add path for local "gen-py/hbase" for the pre-generated module
gen_py_path = os.path.abspath('gen-py')
sys.path.append(gen_py_path)

print "Python & HBase Demo using thrift"

host = "localhost"
port = 9090
framed = False

socket = TSocket.TSocket(host, port)
if framed:
  transport = TTransport.TFramedTransport(socket)
else:
  transport = TTransport.TBufferedTransport(socket)

protocol = TBinaryProtocol.TBinaryProtocol(transport)

# Getting Thrift client instance
client = THBaseService.Client(protocol)

#Opening socket Connection with HBase
transport.open()

table = "tab1"

# Create the PUT call
put = TPut(row="row-1", columnValues=[TColumnValue(family="cf1",qualif
ier="greet",value="Hello")])
print "Putting Data:", put
```

```
# Put Data in HBase using thrift client
client.put(table, put)

# Create the GET call
get = TGet(row="row-1")
print "Retrieving Data :", get

# Retrieve Data from HBase using thrift client
result = client.get(table, get)

print "Result:", result

#Closing socket connection with HBase
transport.close()
```

To run the preceding Python example, perform the following steps:

1. Run Thrift to generate the Python module for HBase as follows:

    **thrift --gen py ../../../../../hbase-server/src/main/resources/
    org/apache/hadoop/hbase/thrift2/hbase.thrift**

2. Create a directory containing the preceding Python program file and the
    directory, gen-py/hbase, generated in step 1.

3. Install the Python thrift library using the following command:

    pip install thrift==0.9.0

4. Create a table called, tab1, with a family called cf1 using the HBase shell.

5. Start the HBase thrift2 server using the following command:

    bin/hbase thrift2 start

6. Execute the program.

The Hadoop ecosystem client

So far, we discussed that HBase clients which work in the interactive mode are
synchronous in nature. For batch processing that runs background work such as
building search indexes, building statistical data for reporting needs, and so on,
a Hadoop ecosystem client such as Hive is used.

The Hadoop MapReduce framework is used to process a large scale of data. For these MapReduce jobs, Hbase can be used in variety of ways such as data source or target or both. This section does not talk about MapReduce usage as it is already covered in the previous chapter.

Hive

Hive is a data warehouse infrastructure built on top of Hadoop. Hive provides a SQL-like query language called HiveQL that allows querying the semi-structured data stored in Hadoop. This query is converted into a MapReduce job and is executed as a MapReduce cluster. These jobs, like any other MR (MapReduce) job, can read and process data other than the Hive table stored on HDFS. In Hive, tables can be defined as backed by HBase tables where the row key can be exposed as another column when needed.

 Get started with the Hive installation, table creation, and data insertion at https://cwiki.apache.org/confluence/display/Hive/ GettingStarted.

Create an HBase-backed table, as shown in the following command:

```
hive> CREATE TABLE employee(key int, value string)
STORED BY 'org.apache.hadoop.hive.hbase.HBaseStorageHandler'
WITH SERDEPROPERTIES ("hbase.columns.mapping" = ":key,cf1:val")
TBLPROPERTIES ("hbase.table.name" = "hbase_tab1");
OK
Time taken: 0.152 seconds
```

The preceding DDL statement maps the HBase table, defined using TBLPROPERTIES, using the HBase handler. The hbase.columns.mapping maps the column with the name ":key" to the HBase rowkey. The optional hbase.table.name map only requires HBase, and Hive has different table names.

To load the table from a Hive table (employee) to an HBase table, use the following code:

```
hive> INSERT OVERWRITE TABLE hbase_tab SELECT * FROM employee;
```

The preceding insert statement starts the MapReduce job and copies the data from the Hive table to the HBase-backed table.

 In the previous insert command, the number of records in both Hive and HBase tables might not be the same, as HBase cannot have duplicate row keys. Hence, the column that is mapped as rowkey to the HBase table always provides the distinct values to HBase.

We can also map the HBase table to a single or multiple (used for distinct column families) Hive external tables (by using external keyword with create statement). In case of table-drop in Hive, external tables are not deleted, rather it removes the metadata information about the table.

Summary

In this chapter, we learned about the different HBase clients that work synchronously such as the REST client, HBase shell, Thrift client, Kundera—object mapper and asynchronously such as Hive.

In the next chapter, we will look into HBase administration and cover HBase monitoring and performance tuning as well.

7
HBase Administration

So far, in the previous chapters, we learned the HBase internals, their usage, and the various available clients of HBase. In this chapter, we will explore the HBase administration concepts, covering the following topics:

- Cluster management
- Cluster monitoring
- Performance tuning

 Looking in depth at each of the preceding topics, this chapter discusses most of the administration concepts theoretically and does not provide the detailed hands-on examples.

Towards the end, HBase cluster troubleshooting is also covered in brief. Let's start with cluster management first.

Cluster management

HBase is a Hadoop-based, highly available, distributed NoSQL database. In a production environment, an HBase cluster is quite responsive to node failures but there are many administration jobs that are performed by the cluster administrator. This job list includes important tasks such as starting or stopping the cluster, upgrading the OS on the nodes, replacing bad hardware, and backing up data. Also, these jobs need to be done properly to keep the cluster running smoothly. Under this section, we will be covering the details of these cluster management tasks.

The Start/stop HBase cluster

Starting or stopping an HBase cluster is a very common task that is performed by any administrator; any kind of configuration change for tuning is a very common scenario. The dependent systems such as HDFS and ZooKeeper are assumed to be running before HBase starts/stops. Apache HBase provides the following script files under the $HBASE_HOME/bin directory to be used for the start/stop operation:

- hbase-daemon.sh: This file is used to start/stop/restart a specific daemon as follows:

  $HBASE_HOME/bin/hbase-daemon.sh [start/stop/restart] [regionserver/master]

  This command needs to be manually executed on each box.

- hbase-daemons.sh: This file is used to start/stop/restart all the daemons as follows:

  $HBASE_HOME/bin/hbase-daemons.sh --hosts regionserversfile [start/ stop/restart]

  This script file wraps the hbase-daemon.sh file and is mainly used to restart all the services on any cluster. This script also requires a password-less SSH from the host running the script to all target hosts.

- start-hbase.sh: This script file typically runs from the master server to start the complete HBase cluster. It wraps the hbase-daemons.sh file to perform this operation. The following command is an example:

  $HBASE_HOME/bin/start-hbase.sh

- stop-hbase.sh: Similar to start-hbase.sh, it stops the complete HBase cluster.

Adding nodes

As the application goes on and the workload increases, the size of the cluster increases as well. Assuming that the Hadoop datanode and region server share the same physical boxes, the following steps are performed to add a node:

1. Start the datanode service.
2. Start the RegionServer service and verify it.
3. Run the "balancer" command on the master server after opening the HBase shell. This will move some regions from all existing RegionServers to the newly added RegionServer and also balance the workload across the cluster.

Decommissioning a node

For a maintenance activity such as a hardware upgrade, node decommissioning is required. However, at the same time, an administrator needs to ensure that there is minimal impact on the cluster availability. To perform this decommissioning activity, HBase provides the `graceful_stop.sh` script under the `$HBASE_HOME/bin` directory.

```
[root@localhost bin]# graceful_stop.sh
Usage: graceful_stop.sh [--config <conf-dir>] [-d] [-e] [--restart [--reload]] [--thrift] [--r
est] <hostname>
 thrift          If we should stop/start thrift before/after the hbase stop/start
 rest            If we should stop/start rest before/after the hbase stop/start
 restart         If we should restart after graceful stop
 reload          Move offloaded regions back on to the restarted server
 d|debug         Print helpful debug information
 maxthreads xx   Limit the number of threads used by the region mover. Default value is 1.
 hostname        Hostname of server we are to stop
 e|failfast      Set -e so exit immediately if any command exits with non-zero status
[root@localhost bin]# 
```

The preceding screenshot shows the usage of the `graceful-stop.sh` script. The `graceful-stop.sh` script performs the following steps in order to stop a RegionServer:

1. Disable the region balancer.
2. Randomly assign the regions from the RegionServer in relation to other available servers in the cluster. It also verifies that the region is copied to the new location before it moves the next region.
3. Stop the RegionServer process.

Decommissioning nodes is an important management task and once the server goes offline, it should be removed from the region server list.

Upgrading a cluster

As Hadoop and HBase are open source, the community brings forth patches and new releases very frequently that contain bug fixes, new features, and performance improvements. For such cases, there is a possibility that new upgrades might or might not be compatible with the existing versions and also might or might not require cluster downtime. When the new upgrade is backward compatible with an existing version, an administrator can upgrade one node at a time without bringing down the whole cluster. This process is called rolling upgrades, as updates are rolled on node by node. During the node upgrade, the cluster is available for use, except for the node that is being upgraded.

The following are the recommended steps to perform the rolling upgrades:

1. Install the new HBase version on all the nodes (do not configure).

2. Disable the balancer process.

3. Decommission the region server gracefully (refer to the previous section). Once done, perform the configuration (setting the class path) if any, with the new version and bring back the server.

4. Repeat the preceding steps for all the region servers.

5. Restart master servers.

6. Enable the balancer process.

7. Run the `$./bin/hbase hbck` command to ensure that the cluster is consistent.

8. Upgrade the client with HBase binaries if required.

By performing these steps, there is much less possibility of facing any issue with the upgrading process.

HBase cluster consistency

HBase comes with a utility called `hbck` to check the region consistency. This utility also runs periodically to keep track of the integrity of the HBase tables. In newer versions of HBase, such as 0.92.2+ and 0.94.0+, this utility is referred to as `uberhbck`. You can run the `hbck` tool to detect inconsistencies, as shown in the following command:

$HBASE_HOME/bin/hbase hbck

On executing the command, the following summary about the cluster is displayed :

```
Summary:
  hbase:meta is okay.
    Number of regions: 1
    Deployed on:  localhost,56149,1405965131802
  firsttable is okay.
    Number of regions: 1
    Deployed on:  localhost,56149,1405965131802
  tab2 is okay.
    Number of regions: 1
    Deployed on:  localhost,56149,1405965131802
  hbase:namespace is okay.
    Number of regions: 1
    Deployed on:  localhost,56149,1405965131802
0 inconsistencies detected.
Status: OK
```

During execution, the hbck tool scans the .META. table to gather all the information it holds. It also scans the HDFS root directory that HBase is configured to use. It then compares the collected details to report on inconsistencies and integrity issues. This tool checks the inconsistency at both region and table levels. The following are the different types of checks:

- **Consistency check**: This check applies to a region. The tool checks whether the region is listed in .META. and exists in HDFS. It also checks whether the region should only be assigned to exactly one region server.

- **Integrity check**: This check is applicable to tables. As per this check any rowkey should be assigned to a single region only.

This utility also provides the facility of fixing the inconsistencies. Some of the flags used to fix the issues are as follows:

- Use -fixAssignments when:
  - Regions are assigned to multiple RegionServers
  - Regions are incorrectly assigned to a RegionServer but are being served by some other RegionServer
  - Regions exist in .META. but haven't been assigned to any RegionServer

- Use -fixHdfsOverlaps when:
  - Regions having overlapping key ranges

- Use -fixHdfsOrphans when:
  - The .regioninfo file stored in HDFS that holds metadata for the region is missing

HBase data import/export tools

HBase deals with lots of data spread over one or more regions and tables. Sometimes, full or partial data needs to be either moved in or out from the cluster either for data backup or data migration to another cluster. HBase comes with utility tools for import and export data that use MapReduce jobs. These MapReduce jobs can be used to write subsets, or an entire table, to flat files in HDFS and also load them back into the HBase cluster again.

The Export job takes the source table name and the output directory name as inputs. The number of versions, filters, and start and end timestamps can also be provided with the export job to have fine-grained control. Here, the start and end timestamps help in executing the incremental export from the tables. The data is written as Hadoop SequenceFiles in the specified output directory. The SequenceFiles data is keyed from rowkey to persist Result instances:

```
$hbase org.apache.hadoop.hbase.mapreduce.Export
```

```
Usage: Export [-D <property=value>]* <tablename> <outputdir> [<versions>
[<starttime> [<endtime>]] [^[regex pattern] or [Prefix] to filter]]
```

The -D properties will be applied to the conf used; for example:

```
    -D mapred.output.compress=true
```

```
    -D mapred.output.compression.codec=org.apache.hadoop.io.compress.
GzipCodec
```

```
    -D mapred.output.compression.type=BLOCK
```

Additionally, the following SCAN properties can be specified to control/limit what is exported:

```
    -D hbase.mapreduce.scan.column.family=<familyName>
```

```
    -D hbase.mapreduce.include.deleted.rows=true
```

For performance, consider the following properties:

```
    -Dhbase.client.scanner.caching=100
```

```
    -Dmapred.map.tasks.speculative.execution=false
```

```
    -Dmapred.reduce.tasks.speculative.execution=false
```

For tables with very wide rows, consider setting the batch size as follows:

```
    -Dhbase.export.scanner.batch=10
```

The Import job reads the records from the source sequential file by creating Put instances from the persisted Result instances. It then uses the HTable API to write these puts to the target table. The Import option does not provide filtering of the data while inserting into tables, and for any additional data manipulation, custom implementation needs to be provided by extending the Import class.

```
$hbase org.apache.hadoop.hbase.mapreduce.Import
```

```
Usage: Import [options] <tablename> <inputdir>
```

By default, `Import` will load data directly into HBase. To instead generate HFiles of data to prepare for bulk data load, pass the following option:

```
-Dimport.bulk.output=/path/for/output
```

To apply a generic `org.apache.hadoop.hbase.filter.Filter` filter to the input, use the following command:

```
-Dimport.filter.class=<name of filter class>
```

```
-Dimport.filter.args=<comma separated list of args for filter
```

> The filter will be applied before renaming keys via the `HBASE_IMPORTER_RENAME_CFS` property. Further, filters will only use the `Filter#filterRowKey(byte[] buffer, int offset, int length)` method to identify whether the current row needs to be ignored completely for processing and the `Filter#filterKeyValue(KeyValue)` method to determine whether the KeyValue should be added; `Filter.ReturnCode#INCLUDE` and `#INCLUDE_AND_NEXT_COL` will be considered as including the KeyValue.

For performance, consider the following options:

```
-Dmapred.map.tasks.speculative.execution=false
```

```
-Dmapred.reduce.tasks.speculative.execution=false
```

Copy table

The `CopyTable` MapReduce job is used to scan through an HBase table and directly write to another table. During this process, no intermediate flat file is created. Using this utility, `Put` is performed directly into the sink table, which can be on the same cluster or on an entirely different cluster. Like the export job, we can also specify the start and end timestamps to ensure fine-grained control over the data. The `CopyTable` MapReduce job is invoked as follows:

```
$hbase org.apache.hadoop.hbase.mapreduce.CopyTable
```

```
Usage: CopyTable [general options] [--starttime=X] [--endtime=Y] [--new.name=NEW] [--peer.adr=ADR] <tablename>
```

```
Options:
 rs.class        hbase.regionserver.class of the peer cluster
                 specify if different from current cluster
```

rs.impl	hbase.regionserver.impl of the peer cluster
startrow	the start row
stoprow	the stop row
starttime	beginning of the time range (unixtime in millis)
	without endtime means from starttime to forever
endtime	end of the time range. Ignored if no starttime specified.
versions	number of cell versions to copy
new.name	new table's name
peer.adr	Address of the peer cluster given in the format

hbase.zookeeer.quorum:hbase.zookeeper.client.port:zookeeper.znode.parent

families	comma-separated list of families to copy
	To copy from cf1 to cf2, give sourceCfName:destCfName.
	To keep the same name, just give "cfName"
all.cells	also copy delete markers and deleted cells

Args:

tablename	Name of the table to copy

Consider the following examples.

To copy TestTable to a cluster that uses replication for a 1-hour window, use the following command:

```
$ bin/hbase org.apache.hadoop.hbase.mapreduce.CopyTable
--starttime=1265875194289 --endtime=1265878794289 --peer.adr=server1,serv
er2,server3:2181:/hbase --families=myOldCf:myNewCf,cf2,cf3 TestTable
```

For performance, consider the following options:

```
-Dhbase.client.scanner.caching=100
```

```
-Dmapred.map.tasks.speculative.execution=false
```

Cluster monitoring

In large distributed systems, an administrator handles the difficult task of being aware of the overall status of the system, as well as knowing about each server separately. In disaster-like situations, it is difficult to know when and how it got started just by looking at a handful of raw logfiles.

HBase cluster (another distributed system running on top of Hadoop) administrators need to continuously ensure that the cluster is up and operating as expected. For such difficult tasks, HBase provides a large number of metrics that provide details regarding their current status.

There are different solutions provided that can be further grouped into graphing and monitoring solutions or both. Here, graphing solutions, such as Ganglia (`http://ganglia.sourceforge.net/`), capture the exposed metrics of a system and display them in visual charts on the basis of time filters such as daily, monthly, and so on. Monitoring-based solutions, such as Nagios (`http://www.nagios.org/`), use the JMX-based metrics API unfolded by the HBase processes. This solution also sends an alert to the administrators in case of problems or failures of any process within the cluster.

The HBase metrics framework

HBase inherits its monitoring APIs from the Hadoop framework and is tightly integrated with Hadoop. Therefore, the HBase metrics framework is another reason that HBase depends on Hadoop. In HBase, every process, including the master and region servers, exposes a specific set of metrics. These metrics are further regrouped for each kind of server and the subsystems within each server.

The HBase metrics framework works by exposing metrics. These metrics are based on the context implementations that implement the `MetricsContext` interface. Multiple context implementations are provided by HBase for the generation of data points to monitor and graph, including JMX and Ganglia. Here is a list of the available implementations:

- `GangliaContext`: This exposes metrics to Ganglia.

- `FileContext`: This writes the metrics to a file on disk.

- `TimeStampingFileContext`: This is an extension of `FileContext`, as it writes the metrics to a file on disk with the added timestamp prefix to each metric emitted.

- `CompositeContext`: This context is used to emit metrics to more than one context such as using Ganglia and file context together.

- `NullContext`: This context is used to switch off the HBase metrics framework. With `NullContext`, HBase processes neither expose any metric nor collect any metrics data.

- `NullContextWithUpdateThread`: The only difference between `NullContext` and `NullContextWithUpdateThread` is that it allows data aggregation so that JMX-based solutions can use it.

The `MetricsRecord` option represents the group of metrics generated for any subsystem of HBase cluster statistics for the master, region server, or any other process. This MetricsRecord group has a unique name and the fully qualified metric is represented as `<context-name>.<record-name>.<metric-name>`.

The container classes inherited from the `MetricsBase` class keeps track of metrics updates and any events. The following list summarizes the available metric types in the Hadoop and HBase metrics frameworks:

- **Integer value and long value**: This tracks an integer and long counter.

- **Rate**: This is a float value representing the number of operations/events per second. It provides an increment method that keeps track of the number of operations and last polled timestamp to track the elapsed time.

- **String**: This is a metric type for static, text-based information such as the HBase version number, build date, and so on.

- **Time-varying integer and time-varying long**: Under this type, context keeps aggregating the value. The metric has an increment method used by the framework to count various kinds of events.

- **Time-varying rate**: This tracks the number of operations or events and the time they require to complete. This is used to compute the average time for an operation to finish. The metric also tracks the minimum and maximum time per operation observed.

- **Persistent time-varying rate**: This is an extension to the time-varying rate metric. This metric adds the necessary support for the extended period metrics; as these long-running metrics are not reset for every poll, they need to be reported differently.

Now, let's discuss the different metrics that are exposed for HBase system components by the HBase metrics framework.

Master server metrics

The master server process is a lightweight process and only involved in a few cluster-wide operations; hence, it exposes only a limited set of information. The following is the list of metrics that are exposed by the HBase master server:

- **Cluster requests**: This is the total number of requests to the cluster, aggregated across all region servers

- **Split time**: This is the time it took to split the write-ahead logfiles after a restart

- **Split size**: This is the total size of the write-ahead logfiles that were split

Region server metrics

In an HBase cluster, region servers are very crucial components that participate in the data read and write path. Hence, it exposes a large number of metrics for each part of the HBase internal architecture. The following list of metrics is provided for detailed information:

- **Block cache metrics**: A block cache stores the loaded storage blocks from the low-level HFiles and are kept in memory until it is full. It exposes the following metrics:
    - Count metric: This is the number of blocks currently in the cache
    - Size metric: This is the occupied Java heap space
    - Free metric: This is the remaining heap for the cache
    - Evicted metric: This presents the counts of blocks that had to be removed from the block cache because of heap size constraints with JVM

- **Compaction metrics**: A region server performs the asynchronous housekeeping task of compacting the storage files. During this process, it exposes the following metrics:
    - Compaction size metric and compaction time metric: This provides the total size (in bytes) of the storage files that have been compacted and the time taken by the compaction operation
    - Compaction queue size metric: This provides the count of files queued up at the region server and waiting for the compaction operation to be triggered

- **MemStore metrics**: Data contained within MemStore on the region server is written to the disk via flush operations. The HBase region server exposes the following metrics for MemStore:
    - Memstore size metric: This provides the total heap space occupied by all MemStores for the server across all the available regions in megabytes
    - Flush queue size metric: This provides the number of regions ready for being flushed
    - Flush size metric: This provides the total size of the MemStore being flushed
    - Flush time metric: This provides the total time taken for flushing the MemStore

- **Store Metrics**: This exposes the following metrics:
  - Stores metrics: This provides the total number of storage files that are spread across all regions managed by the region server
  - File index size metric: This provides the sum of the block indexes for all store files in MB

- **I/O metrics**: The region server provides the following metrics to track the I/O performance in milliseconds:
  - FS read latency: This provides the filesystem read performance, that is, the time taken to load a block from HDFS
  - FS write latency: This provides the filesystem write performance for all writes, including the write-ahead log to the actual disk writing
  - FS sync latency: This provides performance statics to sync the write-ahead log records to the file system

- Other metrics: The region server also provides additional metrics for the total number of read and write operations summed up for all available regions on the region server. The framework also provides metrics for the actual request rate per second and available regions within any region server.

JVM metrics

The primary aim of JVM metrics is to fine-tune the HBase performance. Every HBase process collects and exposes sufficient JVM-related details useful to fine tune the server performance. The following are the different metrics that are exposed under this category:

- Garbage collection: This provides the GC count and GC timing
- Memory: This provides the memory usage by Heap and JVM internal
- Thread: This provides the count of thread in different thread states

Info metrics

Apart from all the preceding metric categories, the HBase metric framework also exposes common informational metrics that provide the fixed information about the different HBase processes such as HBase build data, version, HDFS build date, HDFS version, the user that built HBase or HDFS, and so on.

Ganglia

Like the HBase metric framework, it also inherits direct support for Ganglia from Hadoop.

 Ganglia (`http://ganglia.sourceforge.net/`) is a scalable distributed, monitoring system for high-performance computing systems, such as clusters and grids. It was developed at the University of California Berkeley and open sourced. The Hadoop and HBase communities have been using it as the de facto solution to monitor clusters.

Ganglia has three important components, which are as follows:

- The Ganglia monitoring daemon (`gmond`): This daemon needs to run on every machine that is monitored. It monitors the host and collects the local data and prepares the statistics to be polled by other systems. The `gmond.conf` file defines the properties required for the `gmond` daemon as follows:

```
globals {
user = ganglia
}
cluster {
name = "hbase-Test"
}
udp_send_channel {
host = localhost
port = 8649
}
udp_recv_channel {
port = 8649
}
```

- The Ganglia meta daemon (`gmetad`): This daemon is installed on a central node and acts as the federation node to the entire cluster. It polls monitoring data from running `gmond` daemons within the cluster and saves it as a time-series database. This data can further be used as XML by its own web client or any other third-party client. The `gmetad.conf` file defines the properties required for the `gmond` daemon as follows:

```
data_source "hbase-Test" localhost
gridname "hbase-Test"
setuid_username "ganglia"
```

- The Ganglia PHP web application: The web application comes with Ganglia installation and uses the RRD tool to render the stored time series data in graphs from the central node, as shown in the following screenshot:

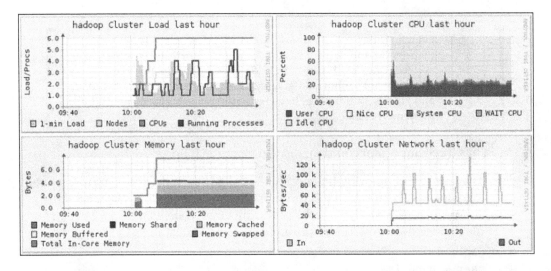

The Ganglia setup is not in the scope of the book. There are many posts available for the Ganglia setup. You can also refer to `http://timstaley.co.uk/posts/ganglia-setup-explained/`.

Once Ganglia is correctly set up, we need to configure HBase so that it exposes metrics to Ganglia. For HBase configuration, set the parameters in the `hadoop-metrics.properties` file, which resides in the `$HBASE_HOME/conf/` directory.

Here, select the context class name based on the selected Ganglia version, and this selection also depends on the HBase compatibility with the specific Ganglia version. If the version of Ganglia installed is 3.1.x, the `hbase` class will be assigned `org.apache.hadoop.metrics.ganglia.GangliaContext31`, and for an older version of Ganglia, its value will be `org.apache.hadoop.metrics.ganglia.GangliaContext`. The `hadoop-metrics.properties` file configured for Ganglia 3.1 or later looks as follows:

```
hbase.class=org.apache.hadoop.metrics.ganglia.GangliaContext31
hbase.period=10
hbase.servers=GMETAD_HOST_IP:8649
```

```
jvm.class=org.apache.hadoop.metrics.ganglia.GangliaContext31
jvm.period=10
jvm.servers= GMETAD_HOST_IP:8649


rpc.class=org.apache.hadoop.metrics.ganglia.GangliaContext31
rpc.period=10
rpc.servers= GMETAD_HOST_IP:8649
```

Once Ganglia is configured with HBase, restart all the HBase cluster processes and Ganglia will pick all the metrics without making any more changes.

Nagios

Nagios (http://www.nagios.org/) is a widely used monitoring and alerting tool for monitoring the entire IT infrastructure. It not only monitors the cluster but also takes actions such as sending emails, SMS messages, triggering scripts, and even physically rebooting the server if configured. Nagios is integrated with HBase using JMX.

JMX

Java applications export their status using the **Java Management Extensions** framework (**JMX**). Open source tools such as Cacti and JMXToolkit (https://github. com/larsgeorge/jmxtoolkit) can be used to collect metrics via JMX for HBase.

 JMX metrics can also be viewed as JSON from the Master and RegionServer web UI, the Master server JMX metrics at http:// master_server_ip:60010/jmx and Region Server JMX metrics at http://region_server_ip:60030/jmx.

To enable JMX accessibility for HBase processes, the following lines need to be uncommented and updated in the $HABASE_HOME/conf/hbase-env.sh configuration file:

```
export HBASE_JMX_BASE="-Dcom.sun.management.jmxremote.ssl=false
-Dcom.sun.management.jmxremote.authenticate=false"
export HBASE_MASTER_OPTS="$HBASE_JMX_BASE
-Dcom.sun.management.jmxremote.port=10101"
export HBASE_REGIONSERVER_OPTS="$HBASE_JMX_BASE
-Dcom.sun.management.jmxremote.port=10102"
```

```
export HBASE_THRIFT_OPTS="$HBASE_JMX_BASE
-Dcom.sun.management.jmxremote.port=10103"
export HBASE_ZOOKEEPER_OPTS="$HBASE_JMX_BASE
-Dcom.sun.management.jmxremote.port=10104"
export HBASE_REST_OPTS="$HBASE_JMX_BASE
-Dcom.sun.management.jmxremote.port=10105"
```

To access any metrics using JMX, enable `NullContextWithUpdateThread` with an appropriate value for the update period; for example, the `hadoop-metrics.properties` file will have the following entries:

```
hbase.class=org.apache.hadoop.metrics.spi.NullContextWithUpdateThread
hbase.period=10
jvm.class=org.apache.hadoop.metrics.spi.NullContextWithUpdateThread
jvm.period=10
rpc.class=org.apache.hadoop.metrics.spi.NullContextWithUpdateThread
rpc.period=10
```

The preceding entries ensure that metrics will be updated every 10 seconds. If some other context is used, metrics values will be retrieved using JMX operations.

File-based monitoring

Like many other ways, HBase can also be configured to output metrics into a flat file. Every time a metric is to be outputted, it's appended to that file with or without timestamps. File-based monitoring is not recommended for production systems. To enable metrics capturing into files, configuration needs to be done in the `hadoop-metrics.properties` file as follows:

```
hbase.class=org.apache.hadoop.hbase.metrics.file.TimeStampingFileContext
hbase.period=10
hbase.fileName=/tmp/metrics_hbase.log
jvm.class=org.apache.hadoop.hbase.metrics.file.TimeStampingFileContext
jvm.period=10
jvm.fileName=/tmp/metrics_jvm.log
rpc.class=org.apache.hadoop.hbase.metrics.file.TimeStampingFileContext
rpc.period=10
rpc.fileName=/tmp/metrics_rpc.log
```

These entries will ensure that the HBase, JVM, and RPC metrics will be captured in files every 10 seconds.

Performance tuning

HBase design and performance is very much dependent on how it is being used with any application. Though all metrics and tools discussed in the previous section provide the system-level monitoring, but this does not ensure that the application accessing HBase is getting optimal performance from HBase. However, monitoring definitely ensures that the statistics help in optimizing the performance, for example, the `Put`, `Get`, or `Scan` performance achieved by the client for any region server, network latencies, number of concurrent clients and many more. All this information actually not only helps to fine tune HBase but also in understanding the client expectation from HBase.

Performance is always measured in terms of the response times of the performed operations. However, this response time is also measured in the context of client's needs; for example, an online shopping application backed by an HBase cluster should get a response in milliseconds, whereas in the case of reporting an application, if the nightly reporting is getting a few seconds more response time by HBase (used as backend), is still doable.

HBase is a distributed database built on top of Hadoop, and its performance is affected by everything, starting from server hardware to network devices used to connect these servers, operating systems, JVM, and the very important HDFS. Hence, tuning HBase cluster performance typically requires tuning multiple different configuration parameters to fit for the application requirements.

Let's look at the areas that require tuning to achieve the optimized HBase performance.

Compression

HBase provides support for various compression algorithms used for the column family. Compression yields better performance as reading large amounts of data puts more overhead on the CPU, compared to compression and decompression of the same dataset. So, other than specific data, such as compressed image, we should always use compression.

Available codecs

The following are the different compression algorithms supported by HBase:

- **Lempel-Ziv-Oberhumer (LZO)**: This algorithm is written in ANSI C and requires Java native interface library for its integration with HBase. This algorithm is highly focused on decompression speed and is also called lossless data compression algorithm. Refer to `http://wiki.apache.org/hadoop/UsingLzoCompression` for further details.

- **Snappy**: This algorithm is developed by Google. In this algorithm, although the compression quality is not that good, the compression speed is very high.

- **GZIP**: Unlike the Snappy algorithm, this algorithm provides very good quality of compression and compressed data takes less disk space but at the cost of compression speed.

Once the compression algorithm is installed, the HBase region server should be configured to test the correct installation at the startup time.

Load balancing

A balancer is an in-built feature of the HBase master that runs based on the value (the default is 5 minutes) provided for the `hbase.balancer.period` property. The main job of a balancer is to equal out the number of assigned regions per region server. It first identifies the regions to be moved, and then it moves the regions to the region server. The upper limit for how long a balancer can run is half of the balancer period.

A balancer can be called from the HBase shell and using the API. It can also be controlled using the balancer switch to change its status to enable and disable.

Splitting regions

In HBase, once the region reaches the configured maximum size (the default is 1 GB), it, by default, splits into two halves. These new parts start taking on more data and grow as new regions. As a negative scenario to this, if multiple regions grow at the same rate, they end up splitting at the same time, which can lead to extreme I/O. Hence, it is recommended to run the region split manually, rather than using it as a default feature. The manual approach provides better control over any available region. To disable auto splitting, simply increase the maximum limit to an extent, say 100 GB, so that it does not trigger frequently and administrates a rebound to perform splitting manually. The region size is defined in `hbase-site.xml`, as shown in the following command:

```
<property>
<name>hbase.hregion.max.filesize</name>
<value>107374182400</value>
</property>.
```

Presplit regions can also be determined based on the largest store file in the region, and with a growing data size, this region will get larger and become the selected candidate for region split.

Merging regions

Load balancing and region splitting are very common approaches for performance tuning in HBase. However, for cases where a large chunk of data is either deleted or there is a requirement to reduce the number of regions on region server, HBase provides a tool that allows merging of two adjacent regions. This operation should only be performed when the HBase cluster is offline. The following is the command-line argument to be executed on any region server:

```
$ ./bin/hbase org.apache.hadoop.hbase.util.Merge <table-name> <region-1>
<region-2>
```

MemStore-local allocation buffers

MemStore-local allocation buffers (**MSLABs**) are fixed size buffers that contain KeyValue instances of varying sizes. As soon as the KeyValue instances are flushed to the disk, the process causes holes in the old generation heap and might cause fragment-related issues. In the case of MSLAB, objects of the same size are allocated from the heap. Once these objects tenure and are collected, they leave holes in the heap of a specific size, and further allocations of new objects of the exact same size will always reuse these holes.

Whenever a buffer is not able to observe a newly added KeyValue, it is considered full and a new fixed size buffer is created. Availability of this feature is controlled by the configuration property called `hbase.hregion.memstore.mslab.enabled`, and the size (the default is 2 MB) of a fixed-sized buffer is controlled by the `hbase.hregion.memstore.mslab.chunksize` property. It also defines the upper size limit (the default is 256 KB) of KeyValue instances that can be stored in the buffer. Instances of larger sizes get stored directly in the Java heap and can again become problematic.

KeyValue instances do not occupy the complete space in any buffer and definitely waste some of the capacity and cause slow performance as well if not used correctly.

JVM tuning

Tuning JVM for garbage collection parameters is a must do for the region server processes as these are the ones handling all the data volumes and I/O. Region servers do not work well with the default setting in JVM, especially with heavy write operations as with such use cases; the MemStores are creating and discarding objects at various stages and the data is collected in the in-memory buffers that get flushed to the disk when the buffers are full.

Depending on the duration of data present in memory, it resides in different locations in the Java heap, for example, data staying for shorter duration usually stays in the young generation (also called new generation) of the heap. However, when the data stays for a longer duration, it is promoted to the old generation heap from the young generation heap. In JVM, the young generation heap space is configured from 128 MB to 512 MB, whereas the old generation heap holds the remaining available heap, which can be GBs.

Hence, configuring both young generation and old generation heap space is very important. The young generation heap should be large enough so that it can hold the objects and the old generation heap can avoid the frequent fragmentation. Wrong configuration of heap spaces can affect the latency of RegionServers as a result of GC pauses. The following are a few of the commands that can use used to fine tune the GC and Heap setting.

- Configure the heap size by editing the `hbase-env.sh` file. For example, the following code snippet configures a 5000 MB heap size for HBase:

```
$ vi $HBASE_HOME/conf/hbase-env.sh
export HBASE_HEAPSIZE=5000
```

- Add the following code to start the **Concurrent-Mark-Sweep GC (CMS)** earlier than the default:

```
$ vi $HBASE_HOME/conf/hbase-env.sh
export HBASE_OPTS= "$HBASE_OPTS -XX:CMSInitiatingOccupancyFracti
on=50"
```

Once this setting is applied across the nodes, restart the HBase cluster. For further investigation, GC logging can also be enabled using the following command:

```
$ vi $HBASE_HOME/conf/hbase-env.sh

export HBASE_OPTS="$HBASE_OPTS -verbose:gc -XX:+PrintGCDetails
-XX:+PrintGCTimeStamps -Xloggc:/usr/local/hbase/logs/gc-hbase.log"
```

Other recommendations

Other than the previously discussed ways of performance tuning, the HBase cluster should be fine-tuned using a different kind of configuration for different types of use cases or workloads such as:

- Heavy write: Data written goes into the MemStore and are flushed to form new HFiles. These HFiles are compacted. As a best practice, flushing, compacting, or splitting should not happen too often as these processes increase the I/O, thus causing the slower cluster performance. Some recommendations are as follows:
  - ° Keep the region size larger to avoid splits at write time
  - ° Keep the HFile size larger to avoid compaction

- Heavy sequential reads—some recommendations are as follows:
  - ° Higher block size to read more data per seek
  - ° Avoid caching on table

- Heavy random reads: Effective use of the cache and better indexing will get higher performance. A few recommendations are as follows:
  - ° Use a higher-block level cache and lower down the MemStore limit
  - ° For better indexing, use the smaller block size
  - ° Use bloom filters at column family level

In the case of mixed use of heavy read and write, all the performance tuning parameters should be given a serious look and would require multiple rounds of tuning to get the optimized configuration.

Troubleshooting

An HBase cluster does not run smoothly and expectedly sometimes, especially with bad configuration. This section covers the troubleshooting tools and techniques in brief for the HBase cluster running with ambiguous status. There are certain tools that are used while troubleshooting the HBase cluster. The following are some of the important tools that are preferred to be known to the administrators:

- `jps`: This tool shows the Java processes running for the current user.

  `$ $JAVA_HOME/bin/jps`

- `jmap`: This tool is used to view the Java heap summary. For example, the following command shows the summary for the `HRegionServer` daemon's heap:

  `$ $JAVA_HOME/bin/jmap -heap 1812`

- `ps`: This tool is used to view the occupied memory by the processes. The following command uses the `-rss` flag to view sort processes in the descending order by their resident set size as:

```
$ ps auxk -rss | less
```

- `jstat`: This tool is used for monitoring the Java Virtual Machine. Run the following command to show the summary of the garbage collection statistics of an HRegionServer process running with the 1812 process ID and take this summary for every 1000 milliseconds:

```
hadoop@slave1$ jstat -gcutil 1812 1000
```

Apart from the preceding tools, there are many common errors that an administrator might encounter in a production environment. A few of them are discussed as follows:

Too many open files error: HBase runs on top of Hadoop that opens lots of files at the same time. Operating systems such as Linux define the limit (the default value is 1024) for file descriptors that any process might open. In case the user's open file count exceeds the OS-defined limit, the following error is visible:

java.io.FileNotFoundException: /usr/local/hadoop/var/dfs/data/current/subdir6/ blk_-34458031297234453 (Too many open files)

To fix this issue, increase the open file count for the user by adding the following property in the `/etc/security/limits.conf` file:

```
$ vi /etc/security/limits.conf
<username> soft nofile 65535
<username> hard nofile 65535
```

Also, add the following line to the `/etc/pam.d/login` file:

```
$ vi /etc/pam.d/login
session required pam_limits.so
```

Once done, log out and log in again as the user and restart the Hadoop and HBase clusters. The upper limit for files can be verified using the following command:

```
$ ulimit -n
```

Unable to create a new native thread error: The OS defines the limits for the use to execute the number of processes simultaneously. With a high load and lower value for `nproc`, the HBase cluster might throw an `OutOfMemoryError` exception as:

DataStreamer Exception: java.lang.OutOfMemoryError: unable to create new native thread

To fix this issue, increase the process execution count for the user by adding the following property in the /etc/security/limits.conf file:

```
$ vi /etc/security/limits.conf
<username> soft nproc 35000
<username> hard nproc 35000
```

Also, add the following line to the /etc/pam.d/login file:

```
$ vi /etc/pam.d/login
session required pam_limits.so
```

Once done, log out and log in again as the user and restart the Hadoop and HBase clusters. The upper limit for files can be verified using the following command:

```
$ ulimit -u
```

ZooKeeper client connection error: ZooKeeper defines the maxClientCnxns property that defines the number of concurrent connections any client might make to a member of the ZooKeeper ensemble. This error usually occurs when running a MapReduce job over an HBase cluster. In the HBase cluster, region server acts as a ZooKeeper client, and if a region server's concurrent connection count exceeds the limit defined by ZooKeeper, the following error occurs:

java.io.IOException: Connection reset by peer

To fix this error, add/update the following property in the ZooKeeper configuration file (zoo.cfg) on every ZooKeeper quorum node:

```
$ vi $ZOOKEEPER_HOME/conf/zoo.cfg
maxClientCnxns=100
```

Restart the ZooKeeper to apply the changes.

Summary

In this chapter, we looked at the HBase cluster administration techniques. We also discussed the different ways to monitor the HBase cluster starting from using the HBase monitoring framework and JMX to third-party tools, such as Ganglia and Nagios.

In the last section, we learned about the performance tuning areas that require considerations to get the optimized performance based on the workloads. This chapter also sheds some light on the HBase cluster trouble shooting.

Index

HLog 55-57
HTable class 28
HTableDescriptor class
  about 86
  HColumnDescriptor(byte[] familyName
    method 87
  HColumnDescriptor(String familyName)
    method 87
HTablePool class 28

I

incr command 97
indexing solutions for HBase approach 40
info metrics 130
interface definition (ID) 112
int getDeadServers() method 92
int getRegionsCount() method 93
int getRequestsCount() method 93
I/O metrics
  FS read latency 130
  FS sync latency 130
  FS write latency 130

J

Java 1.7 installation
  about 9
  fully distributed mode 15
  local mode 10-13
  pseudo-distributed mode 13, 14
Java Management Extensions (JMX)
  about 133, 134
  URL 133
Java Transaction API (JTA) 99
JMXToolkit
  URL 133
JSON format (key-value pair) 110
JVM metrics
  garbage collection 130
  memory 130
  thread 130
JVM tuning 137, 138

K

Kerberos Key Distribution Center (KDC) 61
keys
  about 37
  column Key 37
  row key 37
key-value pair 110
key value 38
Kundera
  advantages 99
  binaries, URL 99
  binaries, using 99
  building, from source 100
  features 108
  filters, using with 107
  Maven dependency, using 99
  used, for performing CRUD
    operations 101-105
  used, for querying HBase 106
  using, ways 99, 100

L

Lempel-Ziv-Oberhumer (LZO) 135
local mode, HBase installation 10-13

M

Main class, implementing
  guidelines 69
Mapper class, implementing
  guidelines 69
MapReduce (MR)
  about 5
  running, over HBase 68-70
Map<String, RegionState>
    getRegionsInTransition() method 93
master-master replication 60
MasterObserver type 83
master-push pattern, designing
  about 59
  cyclic replication 60, 61
  master-master replication 60
  master-slave replication 59

Q

QualifierFilter 49

R

RandomRowFilter 47
read operation 103
recommendations, performance tuning
  heavy random reads 139
  heavy sequential reads 139
Reducer class, implementing
  guidelines 69
RegionObserver type 82
region server metrics
  block cache metrics 129
  compaction metrics 129
  I/O metrics 130
  MemStore metrics 129
  other metrics 130
  store metrics 130
RegionServerObserver type 82
RegionServers 17, 53
regions, HBase
  merging 137
  splitting 136
relational database management system
  (RDBMS) 5
REST client
  about 108
  configuring 65, 66
  JSON format 110
  overview 109, 110
  plain format 110
  REST Java client 111
  XML format 110
REST Java client 111
RowFilter 47
row key 37

S

salting approach 39
scan command 97

scan() operation 41
script files, $HBASE_HOME/bin directory
  hbase-daemon.sh 120
  hbase-daemons.sh 120
  start-hbase.sh 120
  stop-hbase.sh 120
setMaxVersions(int maxVersions)
  method 42
setScannerCaching(int scannerCaching)
  method 43
setStartRow(byte[] startRow) method 42
setStopRow(byte[] stopRow) method 42
setTimeRange(long minStamp, long
  maxStamp method 31, 42
setTimeStamp(long timestamp)
  method 31, 42
Simple Authentication and Security Layer
  (SASL) 62
SingleColumnValueExcludedFilter 46
SingleColumnValueFilter 46
single counters 80
SkipFilter 49
Snappy 136
split command 97
store metrics
  file index size metric 130
  stores metrics 130
String getClusterId() method 93
String getHBaseVersion() method 93

T

table scans, HBase 40-43
tables, HBase
  designing 25, 26
Thrift client
  about 112
  starting 112-115
TimeStampFilter 45
troubleshooting tools, HBase cluster
  jmap 139
  jps 139
  jstat 140
  ps 140

Thank you for buying
HBase Essentials

About Packt Publishing

Packt, pronounced 'packed', published its first book "*Mastering phpMyAdmin for Effective MySQL Management*" in April 2004 and subsequently continued to specialize in publishing highly focused books on specific technologies and solutions.

Our books and publications share the experiences of your fellow IT professionals in adapting and customizing today's systems, applications, and frameworks. Our solution based books give you the knowledge and power to customize the software and technologies you're using to get the job done. Packt books are more specific and less general than the IT books you have seen in the past. Our unique business model allows us to bring you more focused information, giving you more of what you need to know, and less of what you don't.

Packt is a modern, yet unique publishing company, which focuses on producing quality, cutting-edge books for communities of developers, administrators, and newbies alike. For more information, please visit our website: www.packtpub.com.

About Packt Open Source

In 2010, Packt launched two new brands, Packt Open Source and Packt Enterprise, in order to continue its focus on specialization. This book is part of the Packt Open Source brand, home to books published on software built around Open Source licenses, and offering information to anybody from advanced developers to budding web designers. The Open Source brand also runs Packt's Open Source Royalty Scheme, by which Packt gives a royalty to each Open Source project about whose software a book is sold.

Writing for Packt

We welcome all inquiries from people who are interested in authoring. Book proposals should be sent to author@packtpub.com. If your book idea is still at an early stage and you would like to discuss it first before writing a formal book proposal, contact us; one of our commissioning editors will get in touch with you.

We're not just looking for published authors; if you have strong technical skills but no writing experience, our experienced editors can help you develop a writing career, or simply get some additional reward for your expertise.

HBase Administration Cookbook

ISBN: 978-1-84951-714-0   Paperback: 332 pages

Master HBase configuration and administration for optimum database performance

1. Move large amount of data into HBase and learn how to manage it efficiently.

2. Set up HBase on the cloud, get it ready for production, and run it smoothly with high performance.

3. Maximize the ability of HBase with the Hadoop eco-system including HDFS, MapReduce, Zookeeper, and Hive.

Scaling Big Data with Hadoop and Solr

ISBN: 978-1-78328-137-4   Paperback: 144 pages

Learn exciting new ways to build efficient, high performance enterprise search repositories for Big Data using Hadoop and Solr

1. Understand the different approaches of making Solr work on Big Data, as well as the benefits and drawbacks.

2. Learn from interesting, real-life use cases for Big Data search along with sample code.

3. Work with the Distributed Enterprise Search without prior knowledge of Hadoop and Solr.

Please check **www.PacktPub.com** for information on our titles

Big Data Analytics with R and Hadoop

ISBN: 978-1-78216-328-2   Paperback: 238 pages

Set up an integrated infrastructure of R and Hadoop to turn your data analytics into Big Data analytics

1. Write Hadoop MapReduce within R.

2. Learn data analytics with R and the Hadoop platform.

3. Handle HDFS data within R.

4. Understand Hadoop streaming with R.

5. Encode and enrich datasets into R.

Talend for Big Data

ISBN: 978-1-78216-949-9   Paperback: 96 pages

Access, transform, and integrate data using Talend's open source, extensible tools

1. Write complex processing job codes easily with the help of clear and step-by-step instructions.

2. Compare, filter, evaluate, and group vast quantities of data using Hadoop Pig.

3. Explore and perform HDFS and RDBMS integration with the Sqoop component.

Please check **www.PacktPub.com** for information on our titles